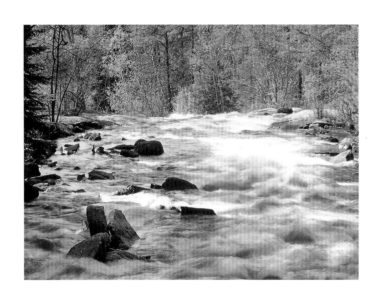

CANADA

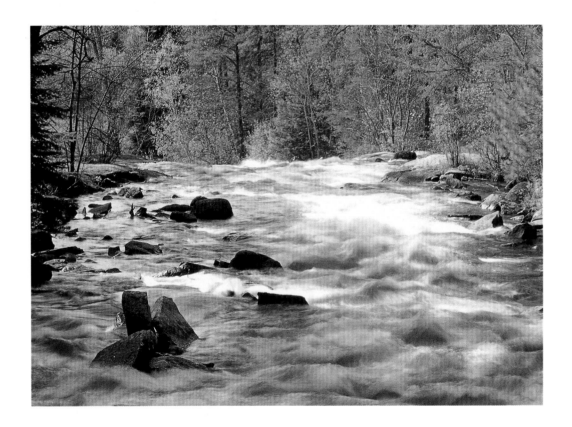

WHITECAP BOOKS

Text by Tanya Lloyd
Edited by Elaine Jones
Photo editing by Tanya Lloyd
Proofread by Lisa Collins
Cover layout by Roberta Batchelor
Book layout by Steve Penner

Printed and bound in Canada

National Library of Canada Cataloguing in Publication Data

Lloyd, Tanya, 1973–

    Canada

    (Canada series)
    ISBN 1-55110-524-1

    1. Canada—Pictorial works. I. Title. II. Series:
    Lloyd, Tanya, 1973

FC59.L66 1997   971.064'8'0222   C96-910739-0
F1017.L66 1997

The publisher acknowledges the support of the Canada Council and the Cultural
Services Branch of the Government of British Columbia in making this publication
possible. We acknowledge the financial support of the Government of Canada through
the Book Publishing Industry Development Program for our publishing activities.

**For more information on the Canada Series and other Whitecap Books
titles, please visit our web site at www.whitecap.ca.**

From Newfoundland's Cape Spear to British Columbia's Long Beach, Canada encompasses almost 10 million square kilometres. And since the Canadian Pacific Railway sent the first transcontinental train across the country in 1886, travellers have been lured by the awesome expanse of the prairies and the foreboding crags of the Rocky Mountains. In *Canada*, photographers have journeyed to the Atlantic, Pacific, and Arctic coasts, capturing the startling contrasts of the land between.

Each of Canada's regions brings images to mind. Prince Edward Island conjures romantic pastoral landscapes while the prairies evoke waving fields of grain. Vast plains of ice and sudden rocky heights mark the giant islands of the Arctic, and the delicate alpine meadows of British Columbia's peaks are known throughout the world. These scenes are beautiful, but they are also rich with cultural significance and historical importance.

From the restored church at Batoche, Manitoba, where Louis Riel staged his rebellion of 1885, to L'Anse aux Meadows National Historic Site, where Vikings settled 500 years before the arrival of John Cabot, this book reveals fascinating glimpses of the nation's past. A picture of Louisbourg brings to life the battles of the eighteenth century, while the totem poles of Ninstints in Gwaii Haanas National Park help to ensure the recognition and survival of First Nations traditions, practised for thousands of years.

These photographs also offer a look at Canada's present and future. The reflection of Vancouver skyscrapers on the waters of English Bay, the off-beat ambience of Toronto's Queen Street West, and the enormous range of the caribou, stretching to the horizon and protected by Ivvavik National Park—these scenes attest to the diversity and strength of this sprawling country.

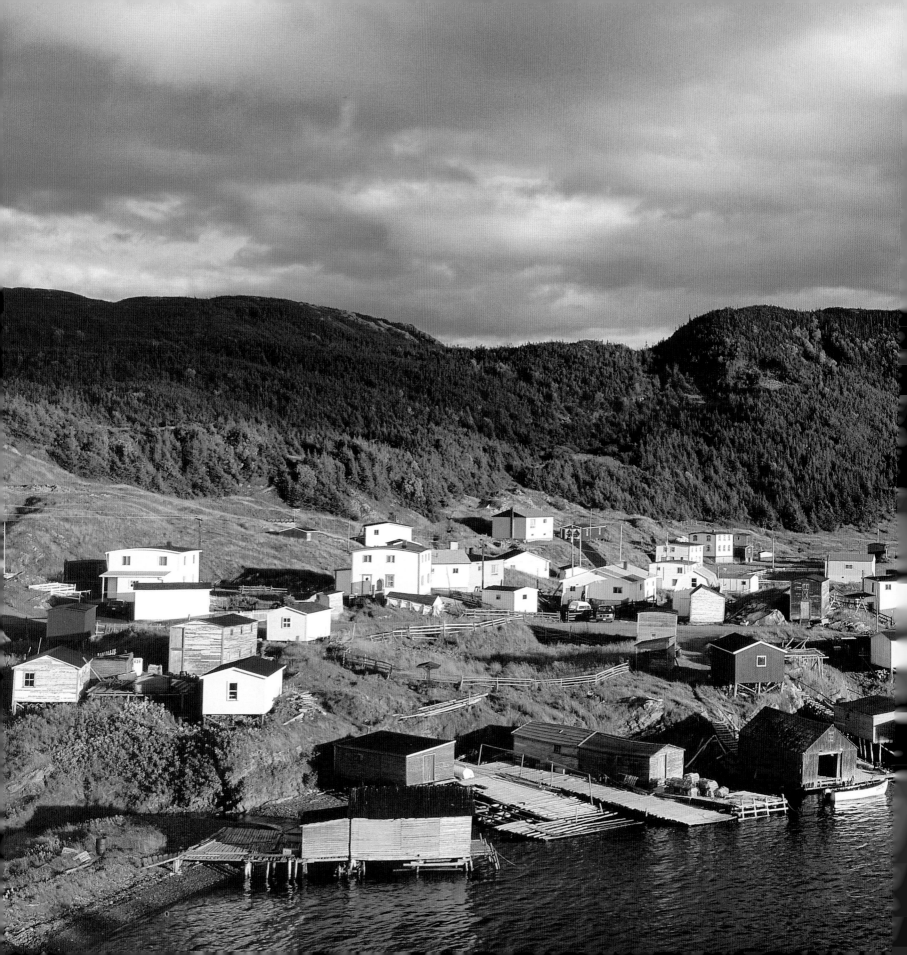

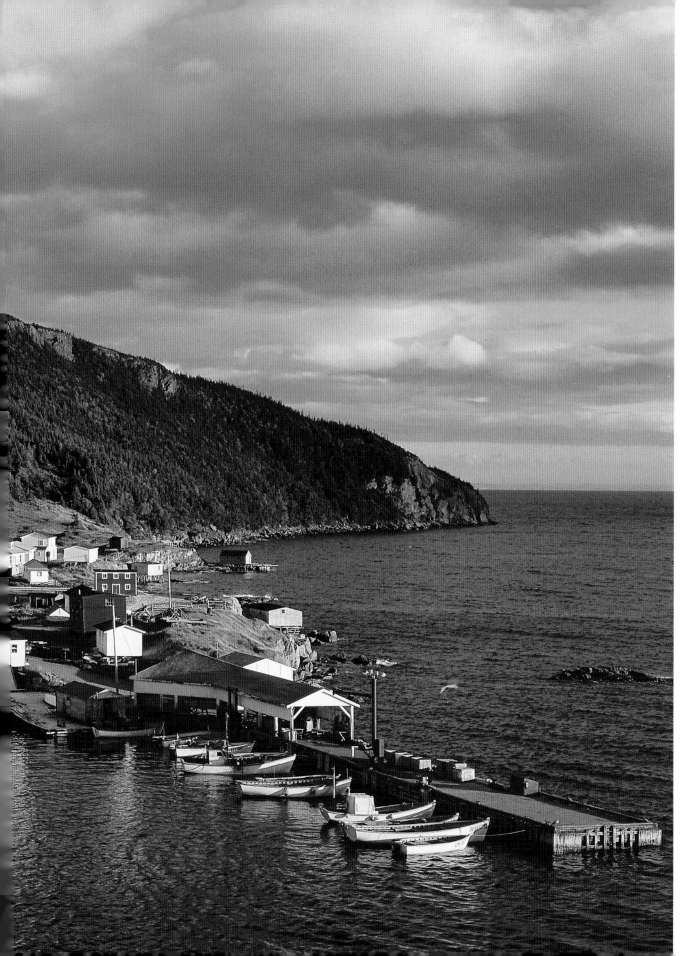

The province of Newfoundland includes the island and rugged Labrador, on the mainland. Though the population is relatively small, Newfoundland is larger than the combined area of the Maritime provinces. Many of its seaside villages began as isolated fishing outports, accessible only by boat.

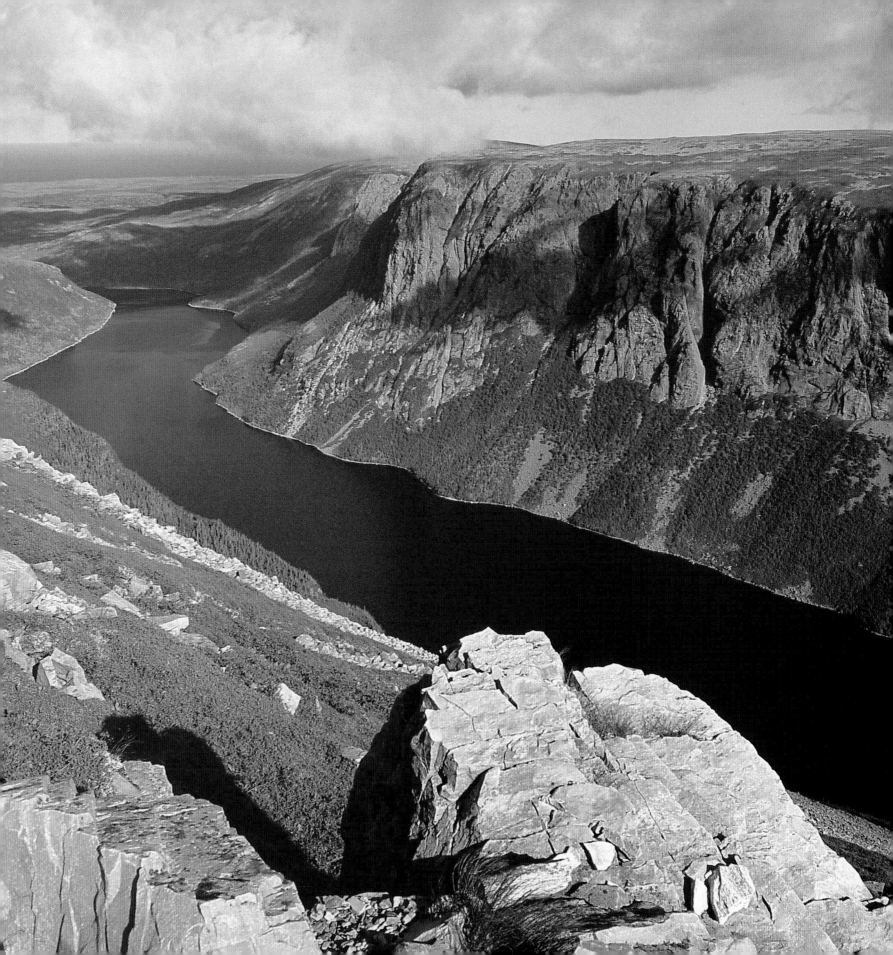

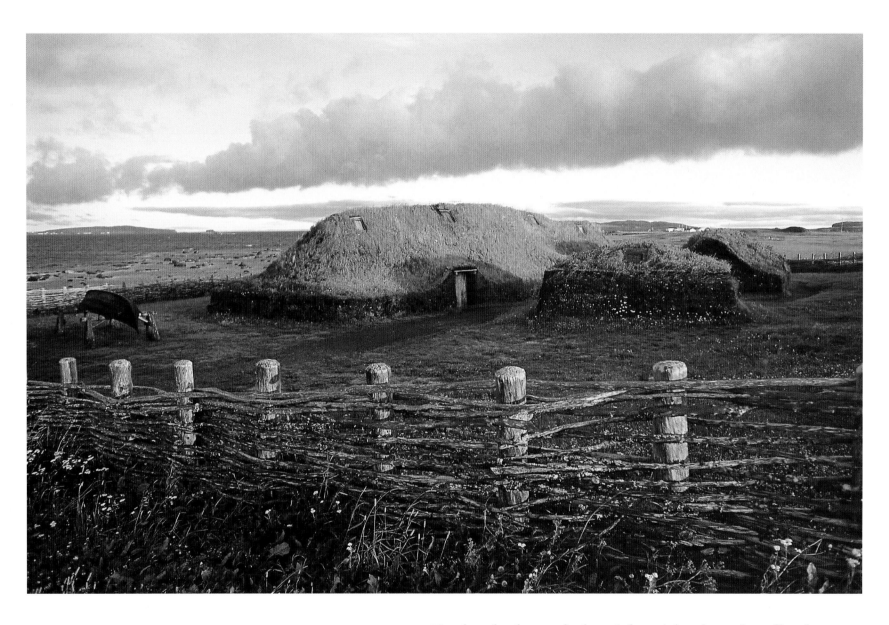

A UNESCO World Heritage Site, Newfoundland's Gros Morne National Park encompasses stony beaches, cliffs, caves, bogs, forest, and amazing fjords. Scientists value these rocky slopes for the evidence they provide about ancient movements in the earth's crust.

Five hundred years before Cabot sighted Newfoundland, Norse sailors and explorers founded a village at what is now designated L'Anse aux Meadows National Historic Site. Archaeologists have uncovered remains from A.D. 1000 and visitors to the UNESCO World Heritage Site can wander through sod buildings and view artifacts and models of the settlement.

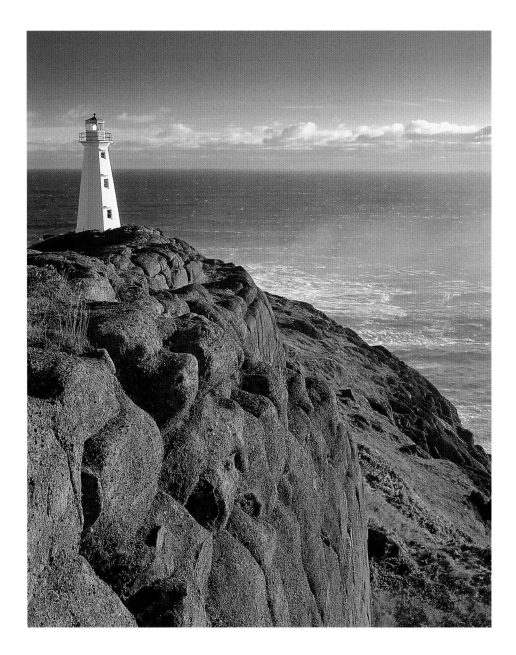

Canada's oldest lighthouse stands 75 metres above the Atlantic on Newfoundland's Cape Spear, North America's eastern tip. It was built in 1836 and used until 1955. The lighthouse keeper's quarters have now been restored as part of a national historic site.

Newfoundland's capital city, St. John's, extends along the protected harbour entrance known as The Narrows. International fishing boats have used the harbour since the sixteenth century. Today they dock alongside drilling ships, military vessels, and luxury yachts.

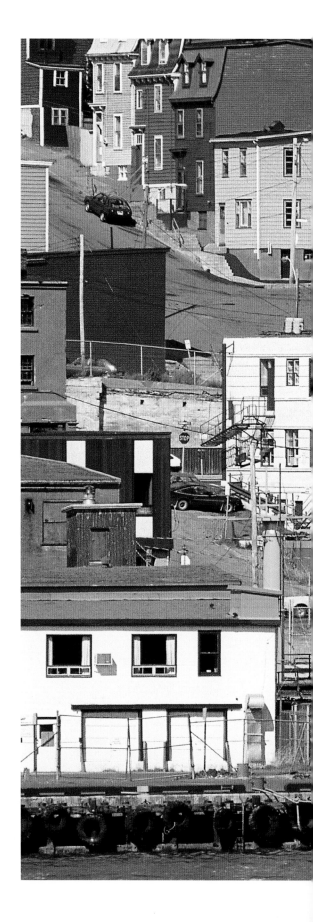

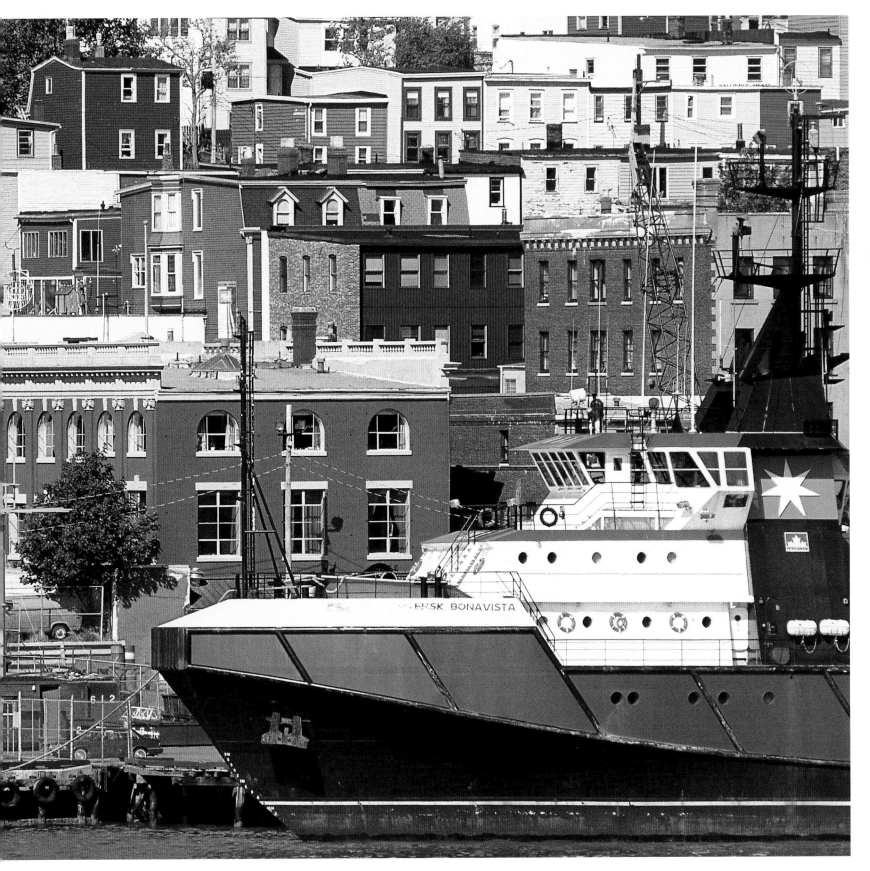

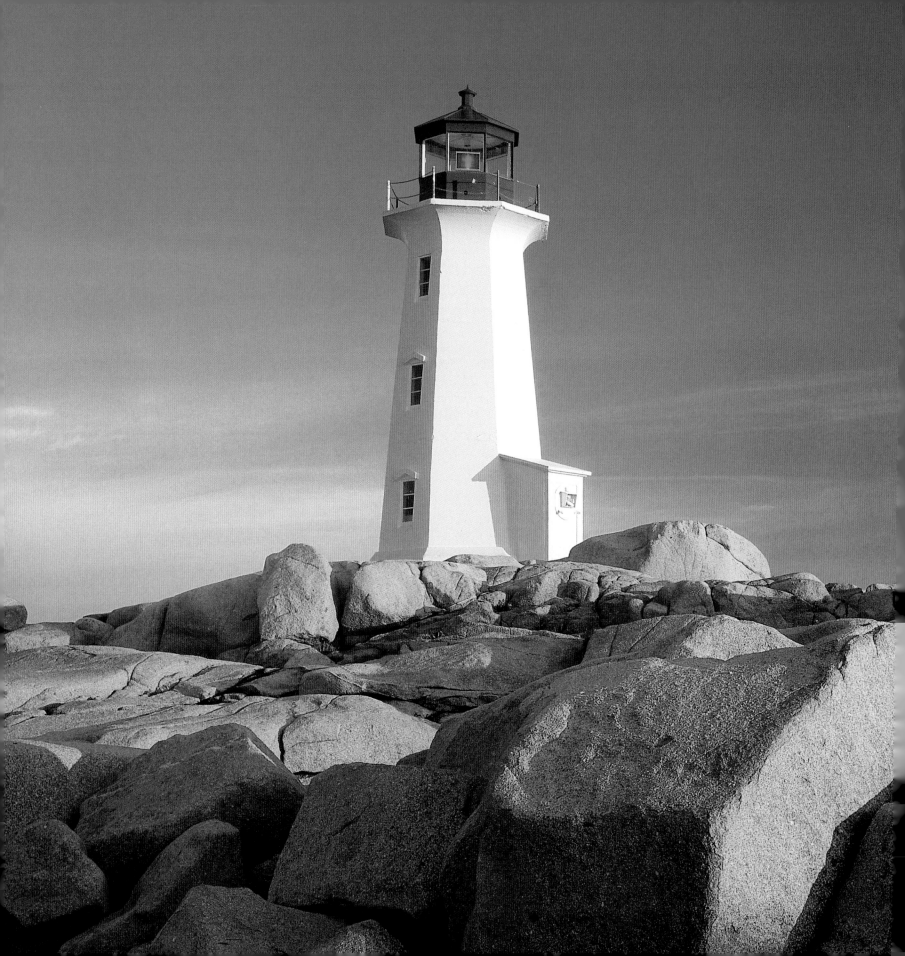

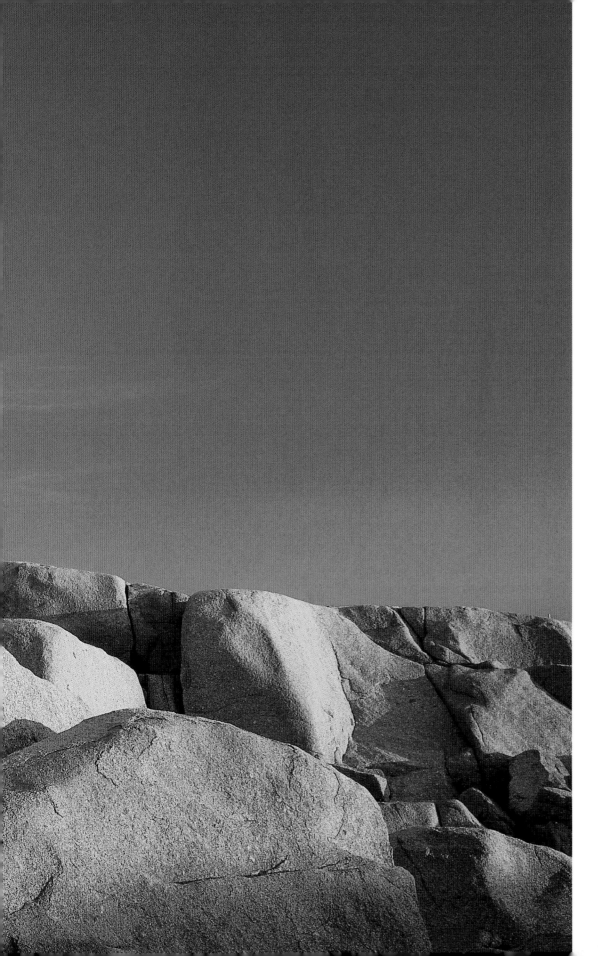

One of Atlantic Canada's most photographed places, Peggy's Cove preserves a romantic view of Nova Scotia's seafaring past. The setting is not so peaceful in a storm—visitors have occasionally been swept off these rocks by giant ocean swells.

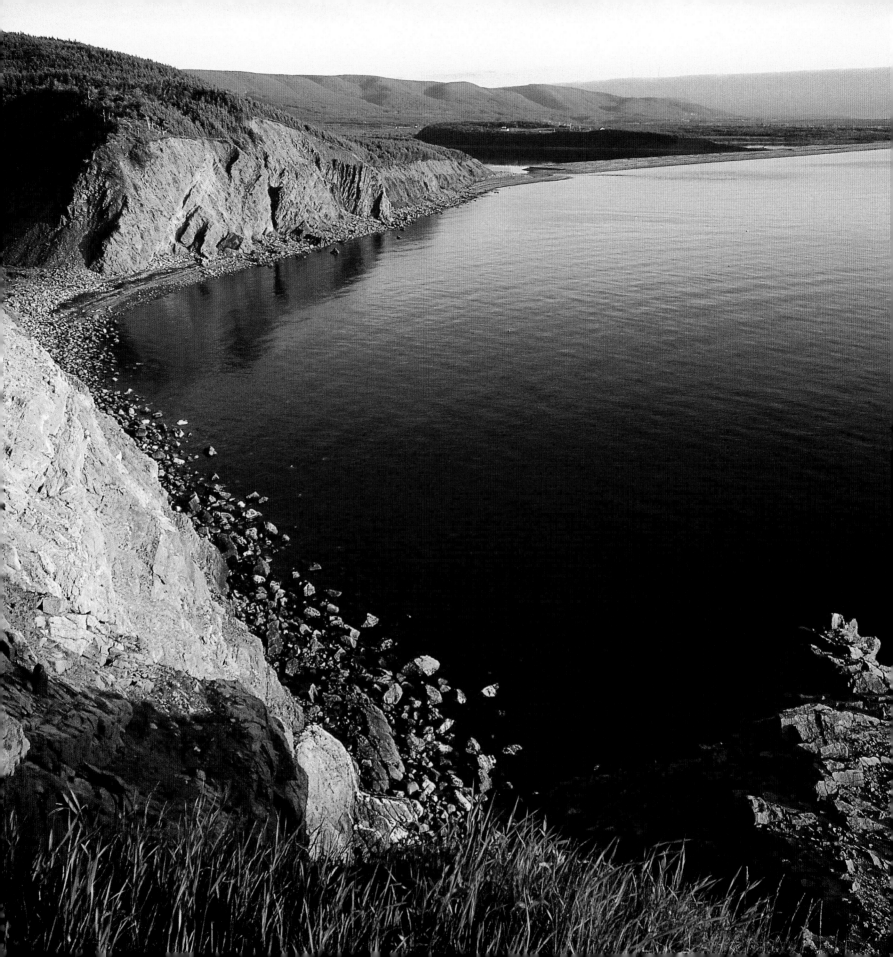

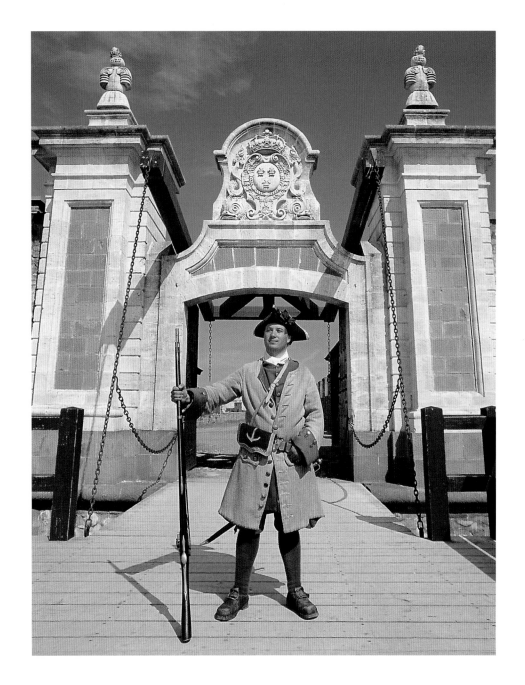

Built by the French, captured by the New Englanders, and destroyed by the British, the Fortress of Louisbourg played a fascinating role in Canadian history. Its destruction in 1760 signalled the end of France's hold on the colony. The Cape Breton Island fortress has been rebuilt and is now a national historic site.

The rugged scenery of Cape Breton Highlands National Park can be seen from one of 30 hiking trails or glimpsed from the 294-kilometre-long Cabot Trail, one of Canada's most dramatic highways. Most of the park is a high boreal plateau, home to lynx, deer, bears, and more than 200 bird species.

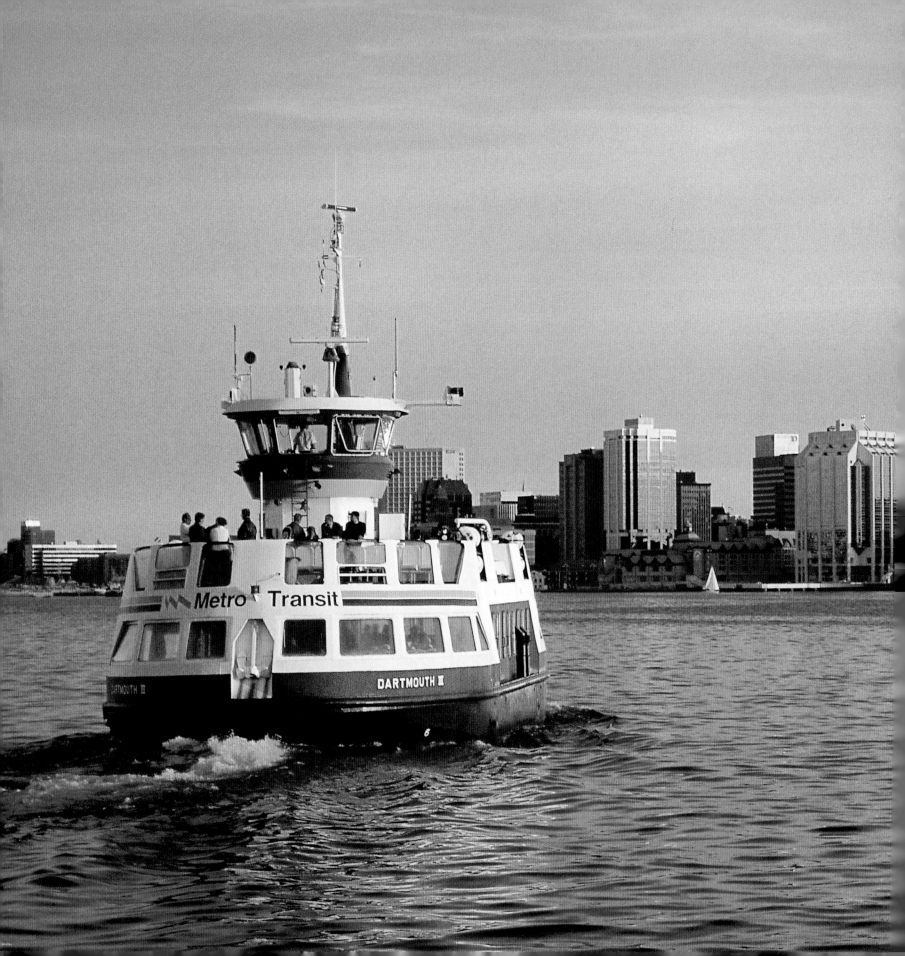

A passenger ferry shuttles commuters and visitors from Dartmouth across the harbour to Halifax, Nova Scotia's capital city. The buildings surrounding the harbour were destroyed in 1917 when a French munitions ship exploded. The largest non-nuclear explosion in history, it killed about 2000 people.

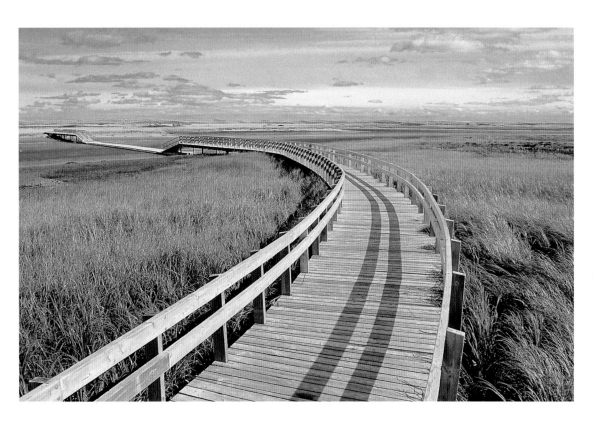

A boardwalk helps protect the delicate balance between wildlife and visitors at New Brunswick's Kouchibouguac National Park. The region's lagoons, sand dunes, and saltwater marshes are important nesting grounds for the endangered piping plover and the park's symbol, the osprey. *Kouchibouguac* is a Micmac word meaning "river of the long tides."

Though the landscape of the St. John River Valley changed dramatically with the construction of the Mactaquac Dam, the river, lined with farms and forest, remains one of New Brunswick's most popular destinations for canoeists and anglers.

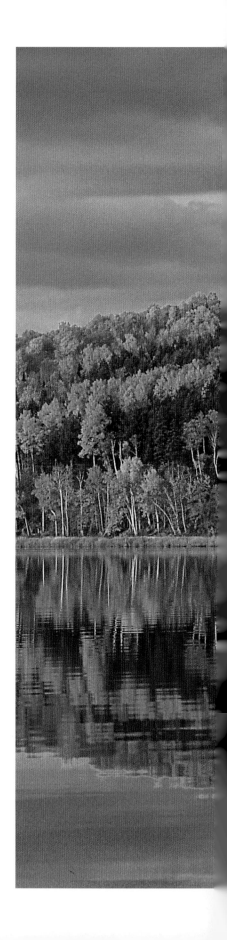

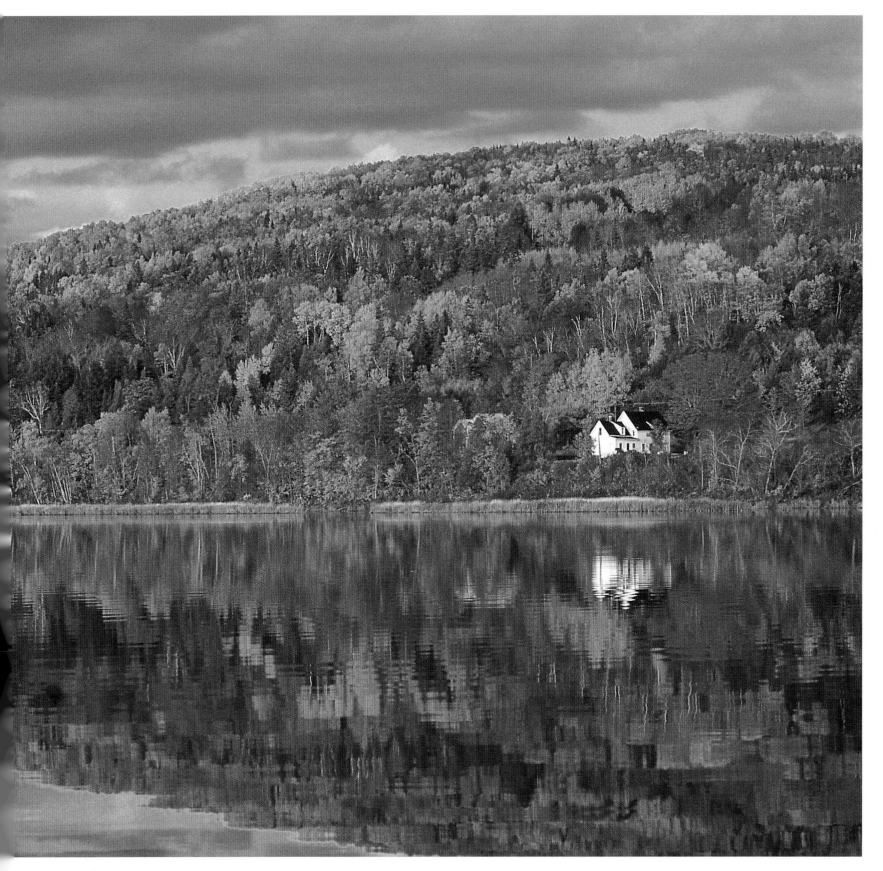

The seabed around New Brunswick's Grand Manan Island is strewn with sunken ships, caught in the treacherous currents caused by high tides. Swallowtail Lighthouse is one of four beacons that warn approaching vessels of the danger.

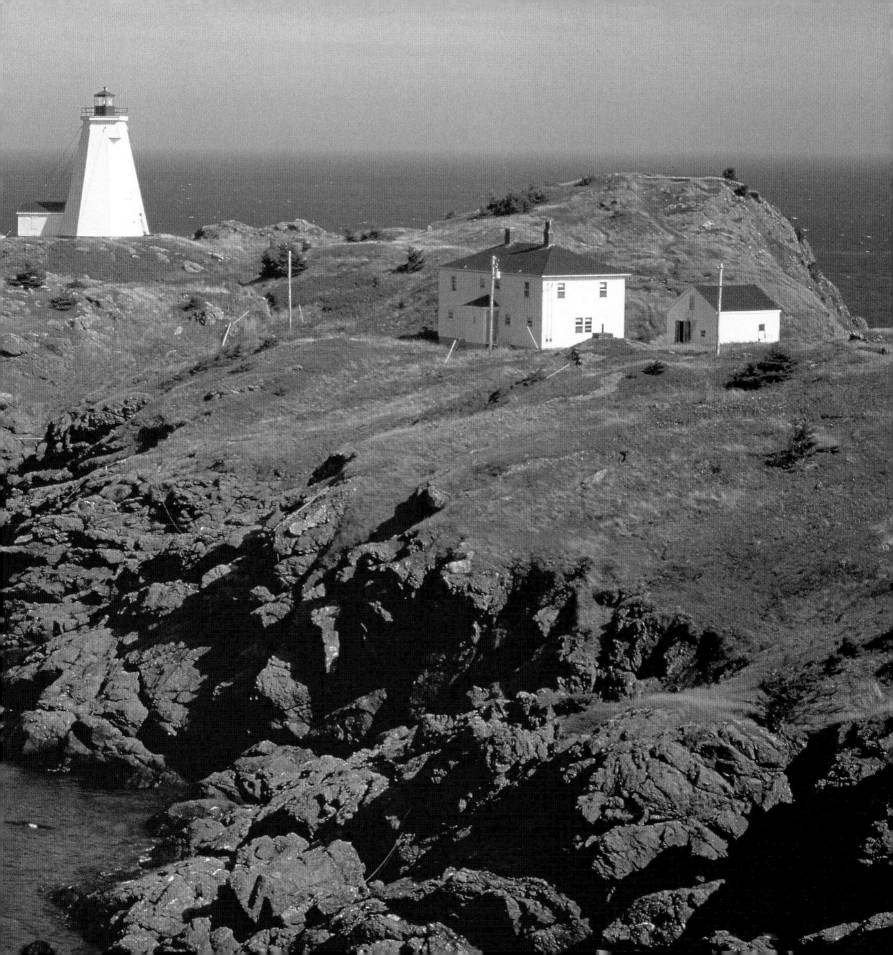

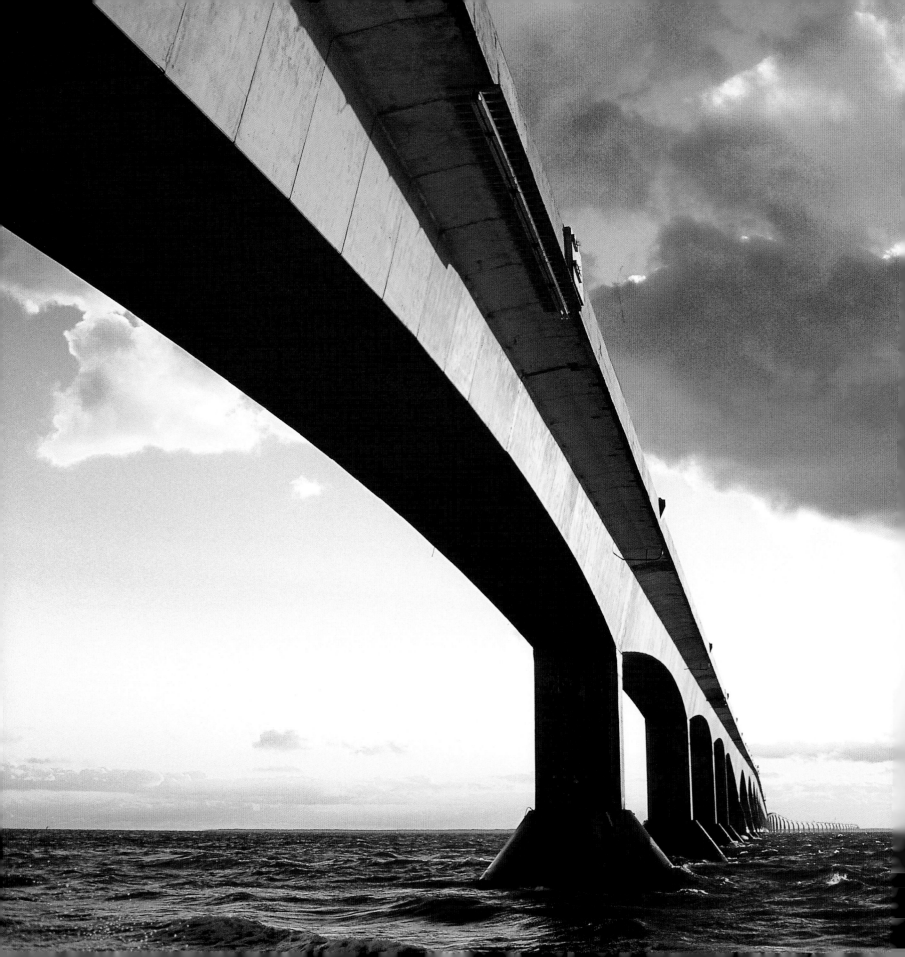

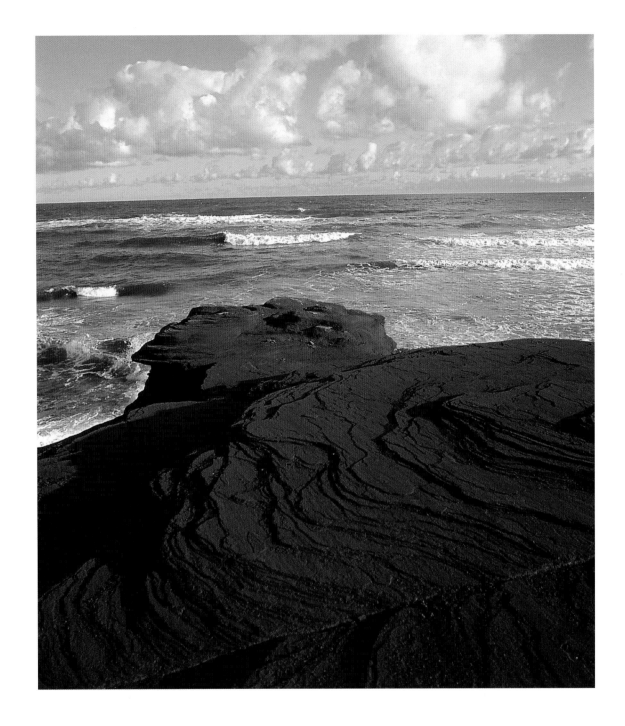

Atlantic swells have sculpted the shores of Prince Edward Island National Park to create jagged red sandstone cliffs and arresting rock formations. The park stretches for 40 kilometres along the province's west coast.

Confederation Bridge stretches 13 kilometres from New Brunswick to Prince Edward Island. The decision to build it was highly controversial, pitting environmentalists against businesses and travellers in favour of the bridge's convenience.

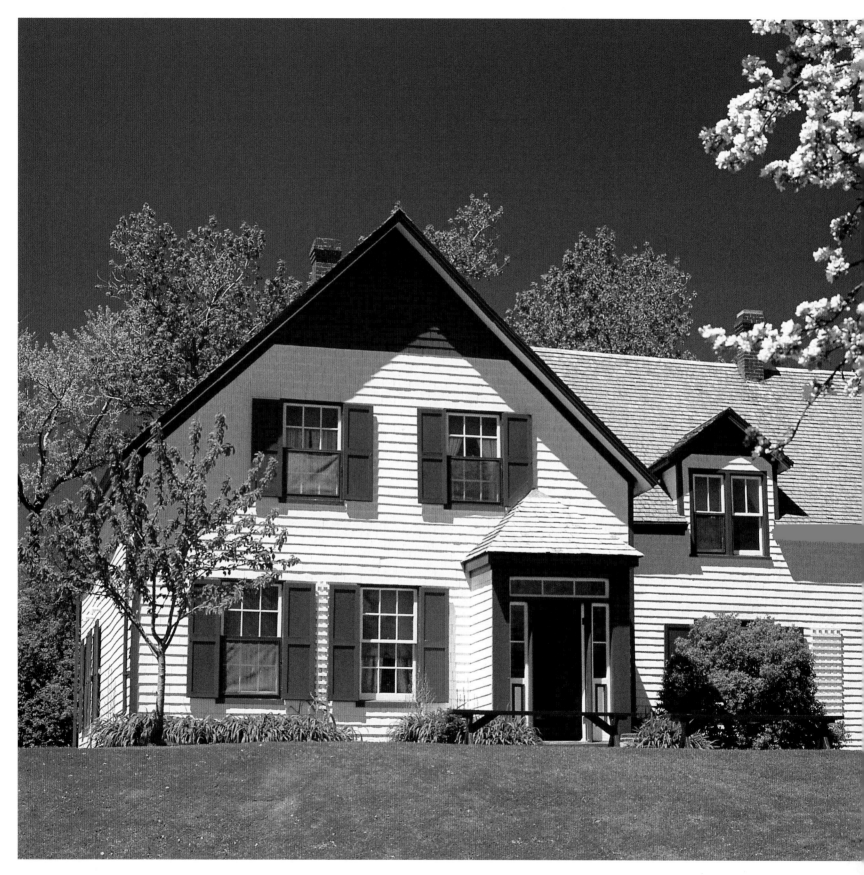

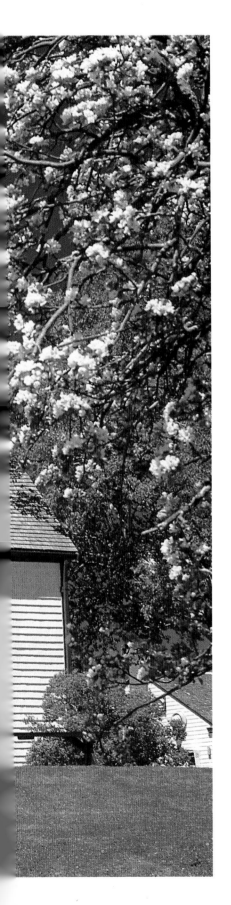

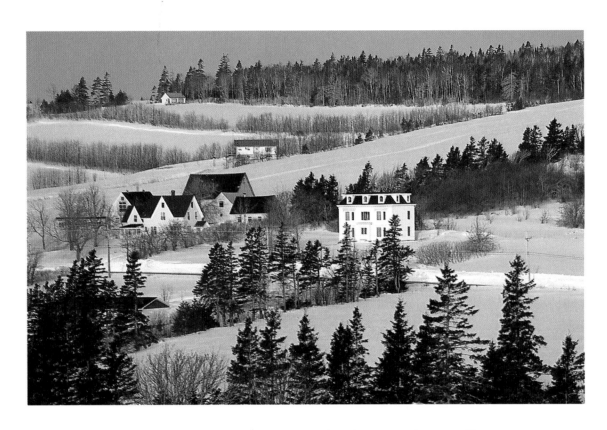

About 225 kilometres long, Prince Edward Island is Canada's smallest province. Fishing and agriculture combine with tourism to support the island's economy. Picturesque farmhouses such as these ones, now blanketed in snow, often host visitors during the summer.

Green Gables House in Cavendish, Prince Edward Island, was the setting for L. M. Montgomery's *Anne of Green Gables*, a novel inspired by the author's own experiences as an orphan. Since it was published in 1908, the novel has been translated into about 20 languages, and read by millions of children and adults around the world.

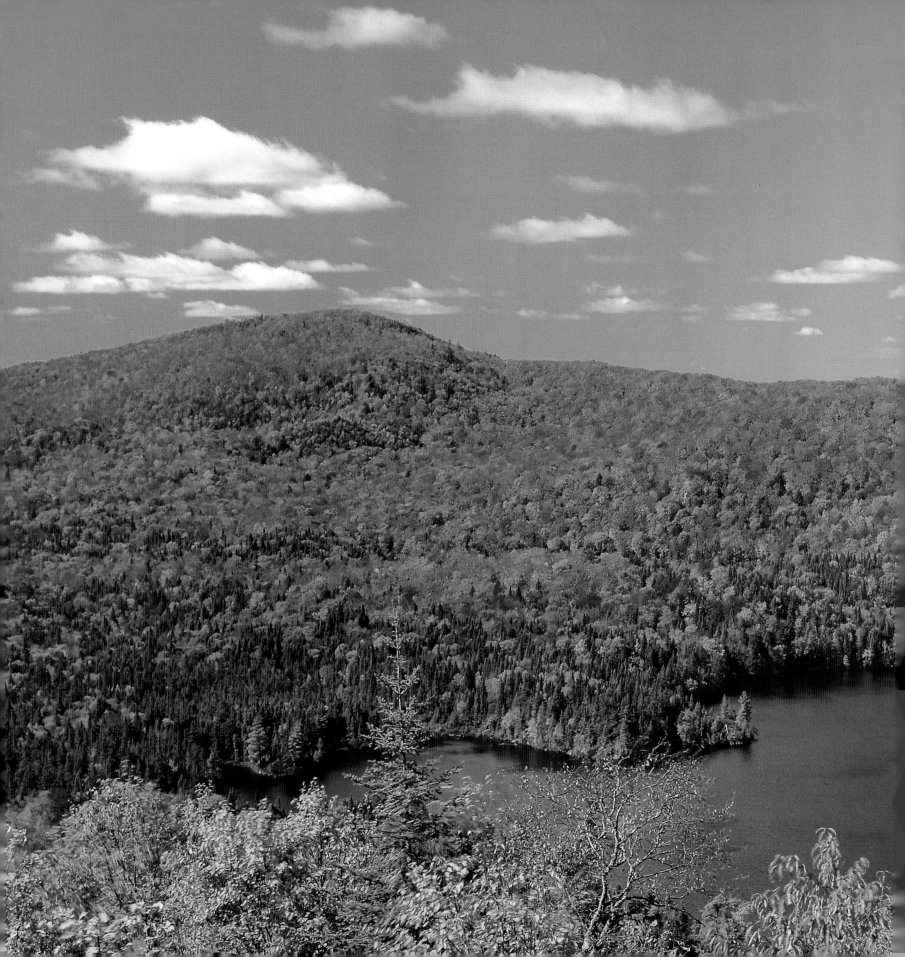

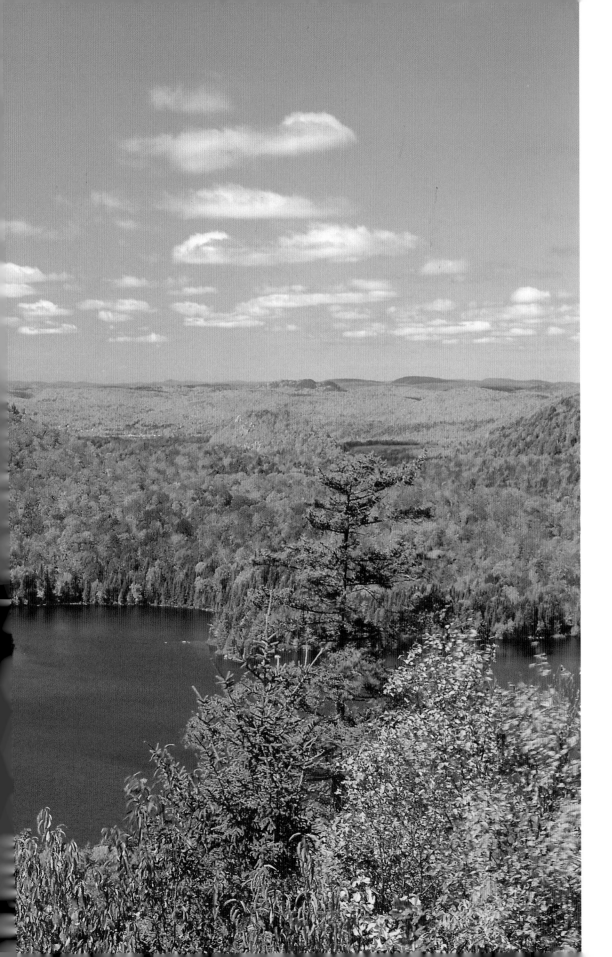

Resorts and outdoor getaways are scattered through Quebec's Laurentian region, where maple, birch, and aspen trees display a dazzling array of fall colour. Canada's largest province, Quebec covers 1,550,000 square kilometres, from the arctic tundra at Hudson Bay to these deciduous forests along the United States border.

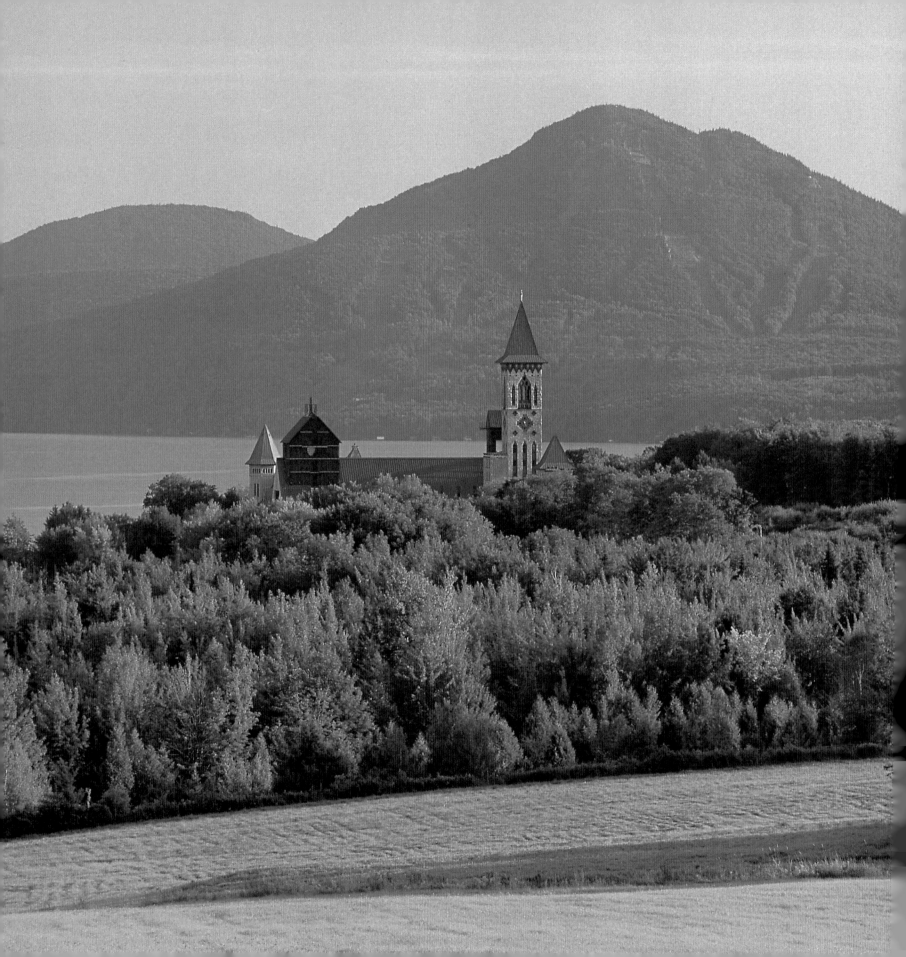

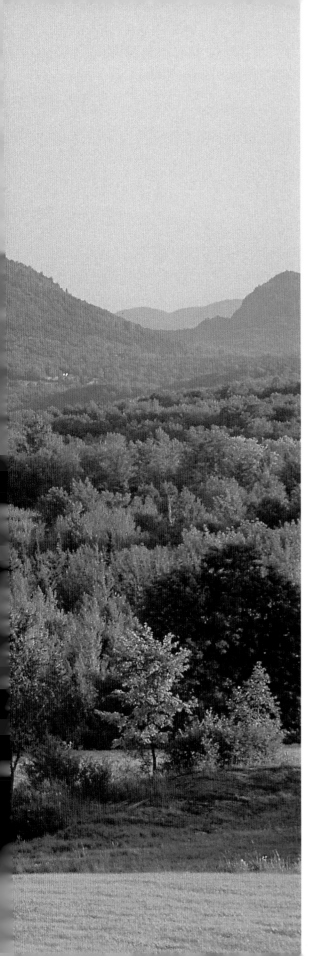

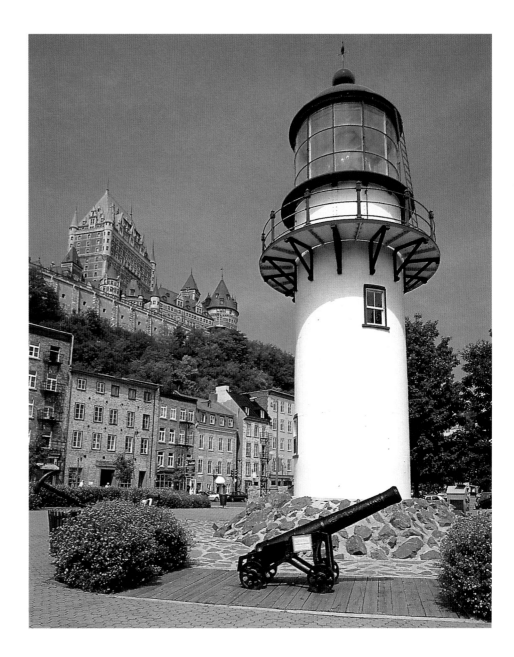

In 1985, UNESCO named Quebec City the continent's first world heritage site. The oldest quarter, the Haute-Ville, is the only walled city remaining in North America. Many of the stone buildings were built in the seventeenth and eighteenth centuries.

The Abbey de Saint-Benoît-du-Lac, southwest of Sherbrooke in Quebec's Eastern Townships, was founded by Benedictine monks in the early 1900s. Evening visitors may be greeted by the low, soothing sound of Gregorian chants.

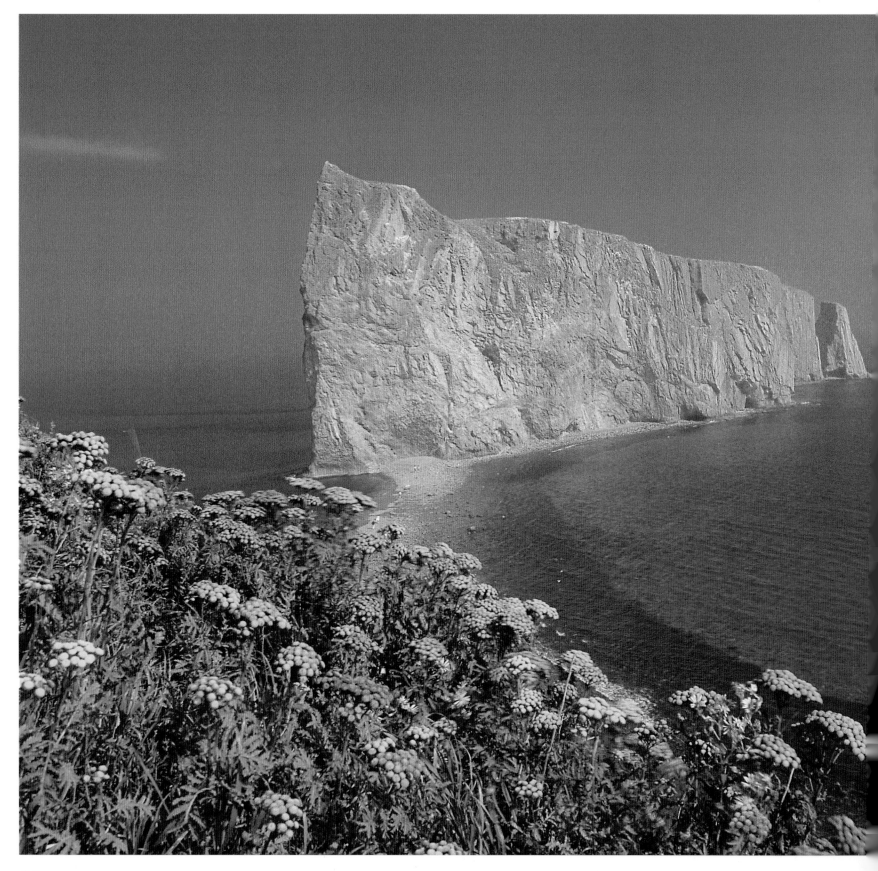

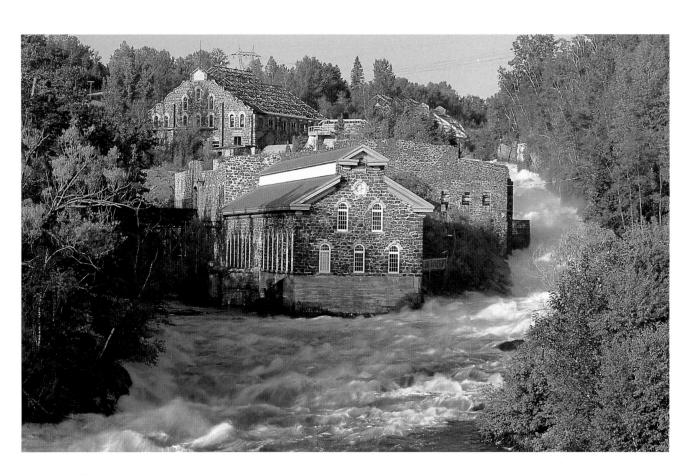

The Vieille Puplerie in Chicoutimi, Quebec, is a unique example of an industrial site turned cultural venue. In the early 1900s, this complex supplied Canada, the United States, Great Britain, and France with pulp and paper. Today, the stone structures serve as outdoor stages.

Pierced Rock, or Rocher Percé, is 88 metres high and stretches for 400 metres along the shore of Quebec's Gaspé Peninsula. At low tide, a sand bar is exposed and visitors can walk to the rock and discover ancient fossils embedded in the limestone.

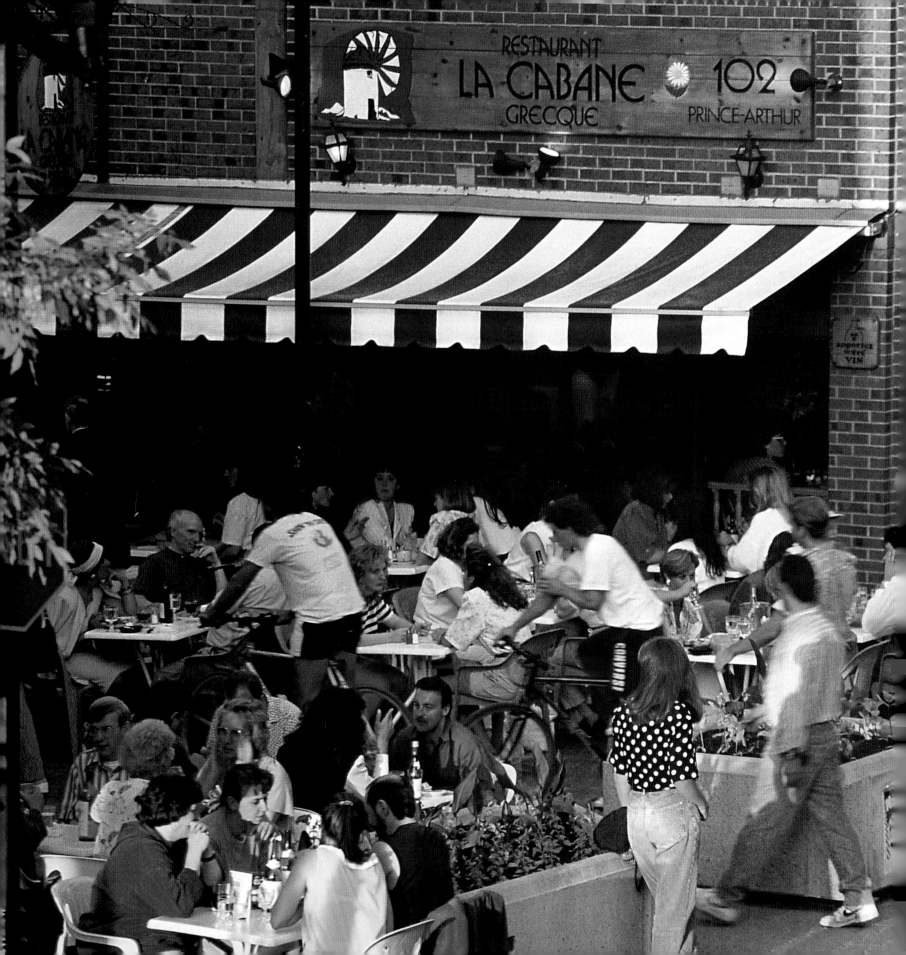

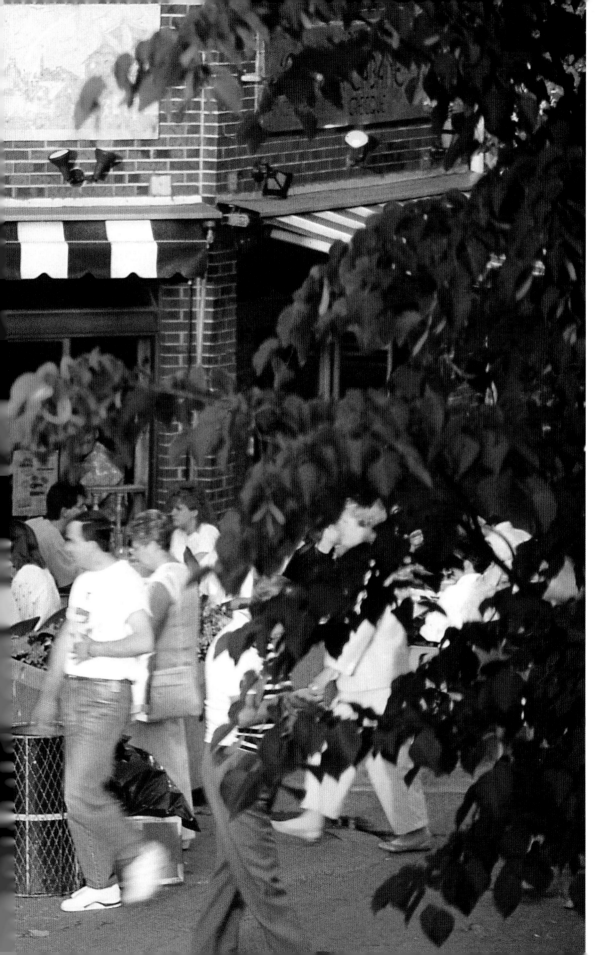

Montreal is a gourmand's paradise. There are more than 4000 restaurants in the city, serving everything from hot dogs to haute cuisine. Rue Prince Arthur, once the centre of the 1960s hippie culture, is now a jumble of ethnic restaurants and unique shops.

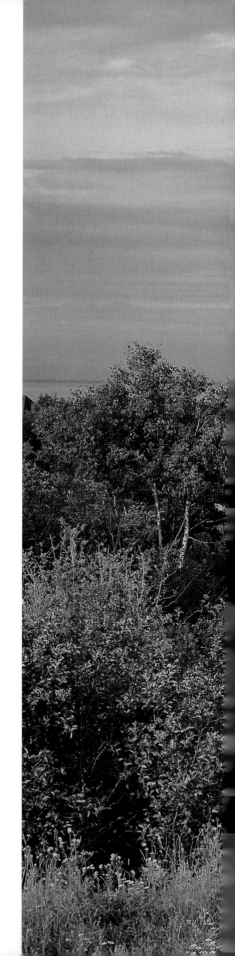

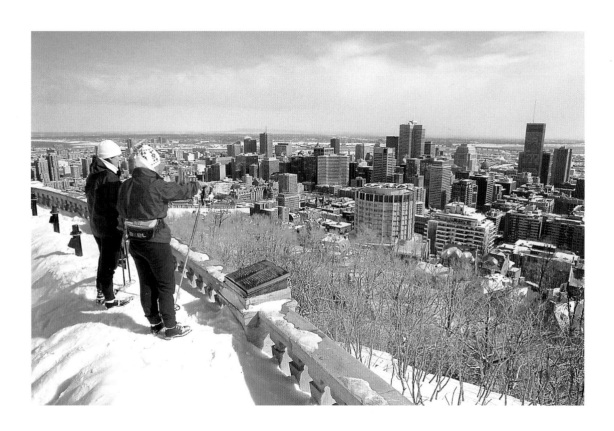

Montreal is named for 233-metre Mont Royal, rising above the
island city. Once the site of a thriving First Nations settlement,
the island became a Christian outpost with the arrival of French
missionaries in the seventeenth century.

Ile aux Coudres on the St. Lawrence River in the
Charlevoix region was settled by the French in
the early 1700s. Though once a base for whale
hunting, the island is now mainly quiet farmland.

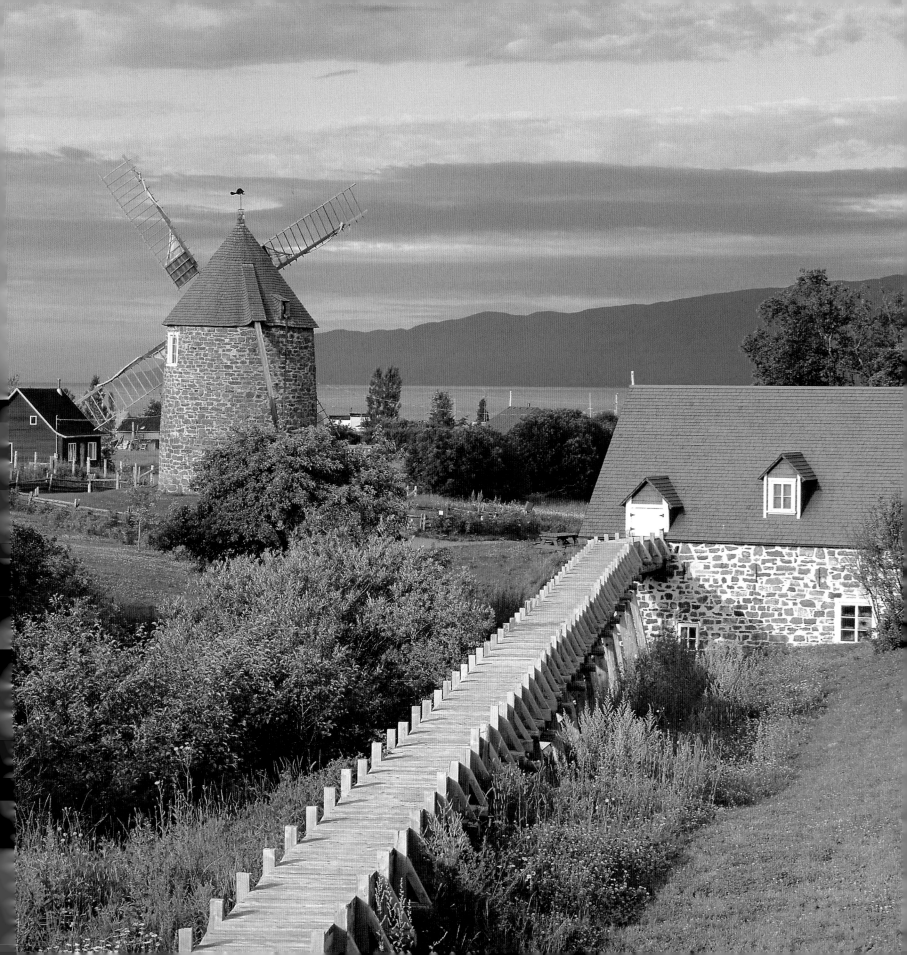

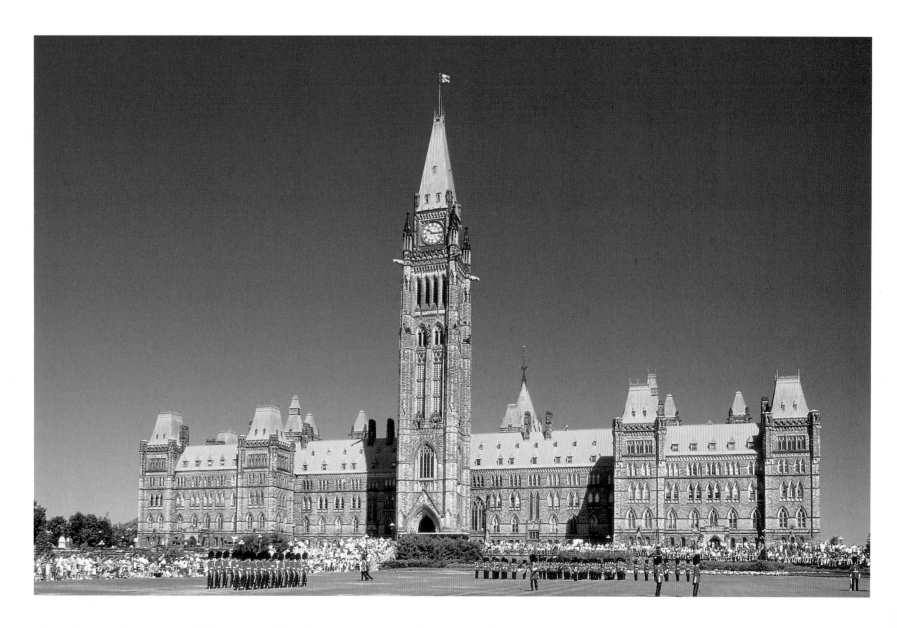

Canada's Parliament Buildings stand high on Ottawa's Parliament Hill, overlooking the Ottawa River. When Thomas Fuller and Chilion Jones designed the buildings in 1859, the Gothic Revival-style arches were lined with eye-catching red sandstone. When the structure was rebuilt after a fire in 1916, architects followed a similar but less colourful style.

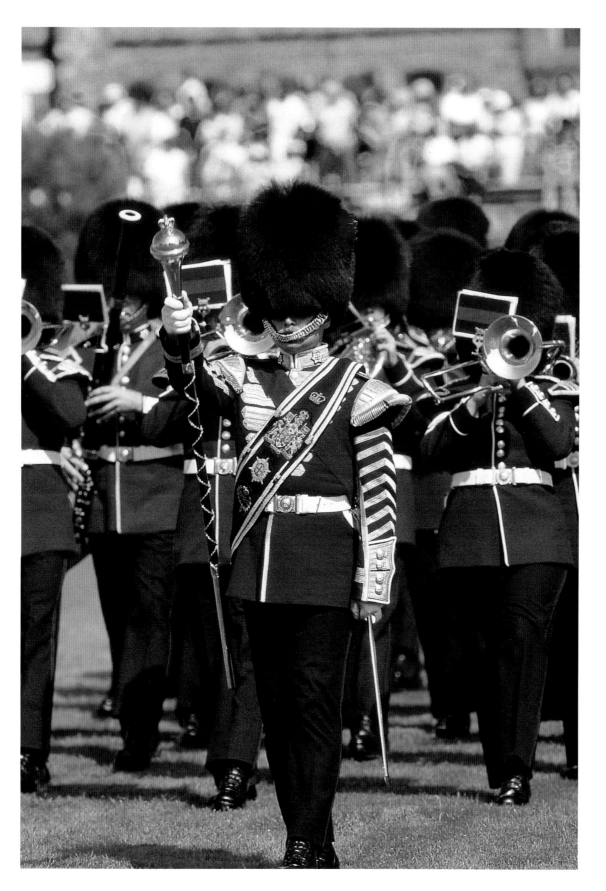

A band accompanies the Governor General's Foot Guards and the Canadian Grenadier Guards as they march from the governor general's residence to Parliament Hill in preparation for the Changing of the Guard ceremony. Held each summer morning, the ceremony includes dress and weapons inspections, parading of the colours, and the exchange of compliments between the old and new guards.

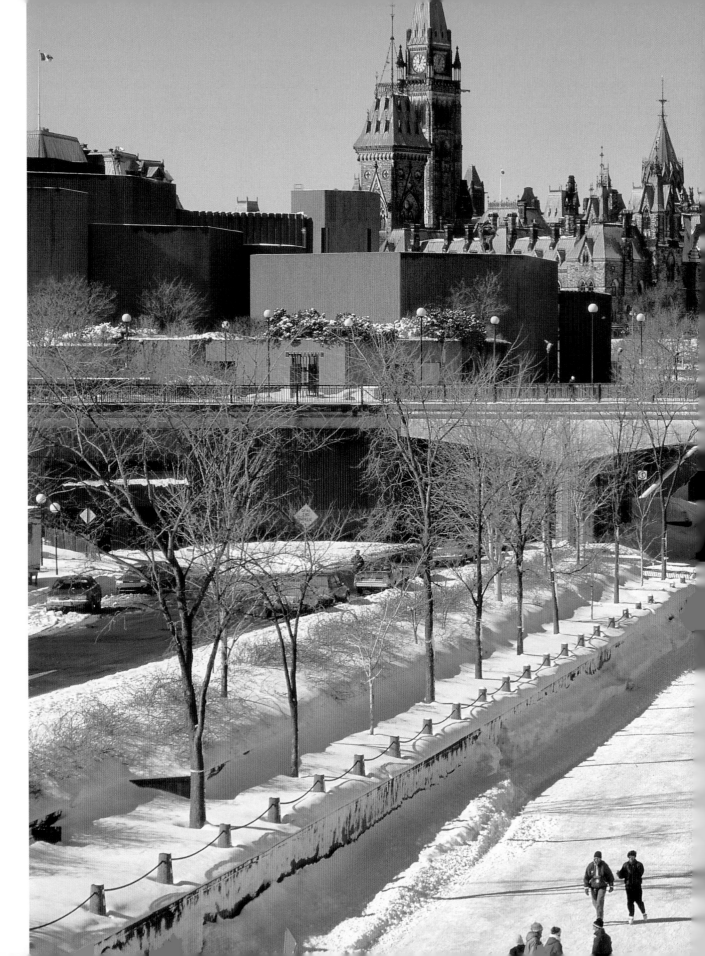

In winter Ottawa's Rideau Canal is transformed into the world's longest skating rink, with eight kilometres of cleared and maintained ice. Each February, the canal is lined with snow sculptures and ice sculptures, part of the annual Winterlude festivities.

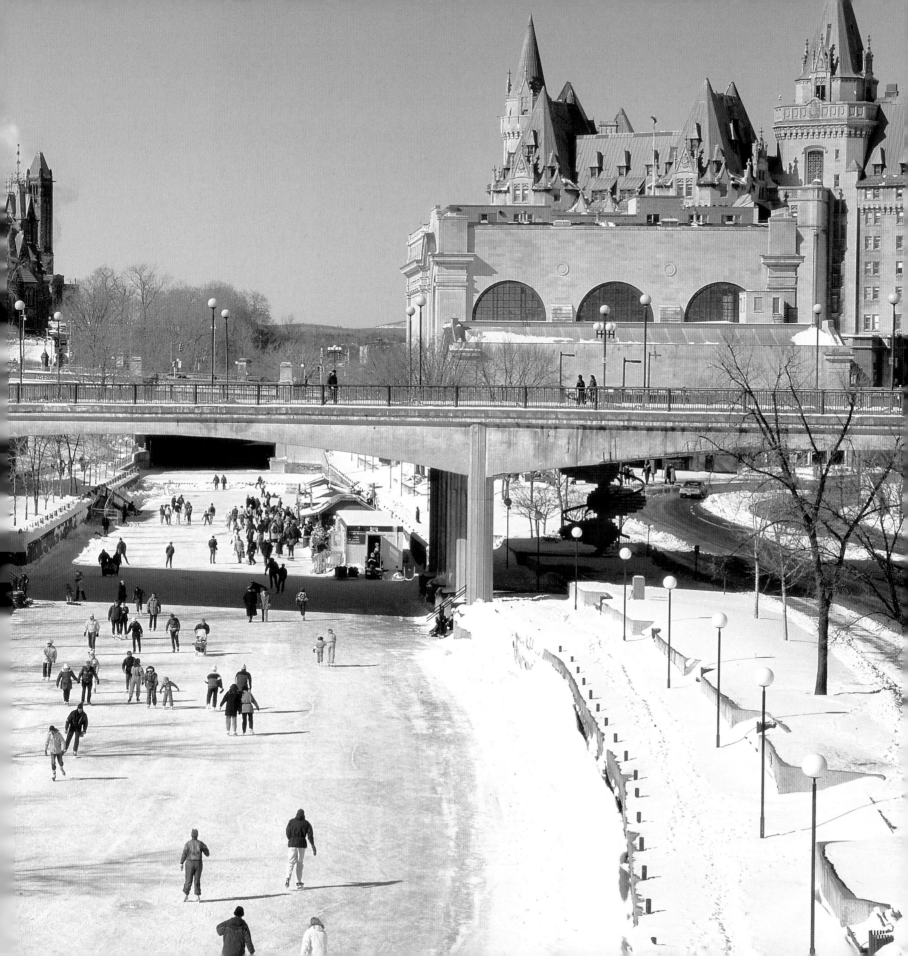

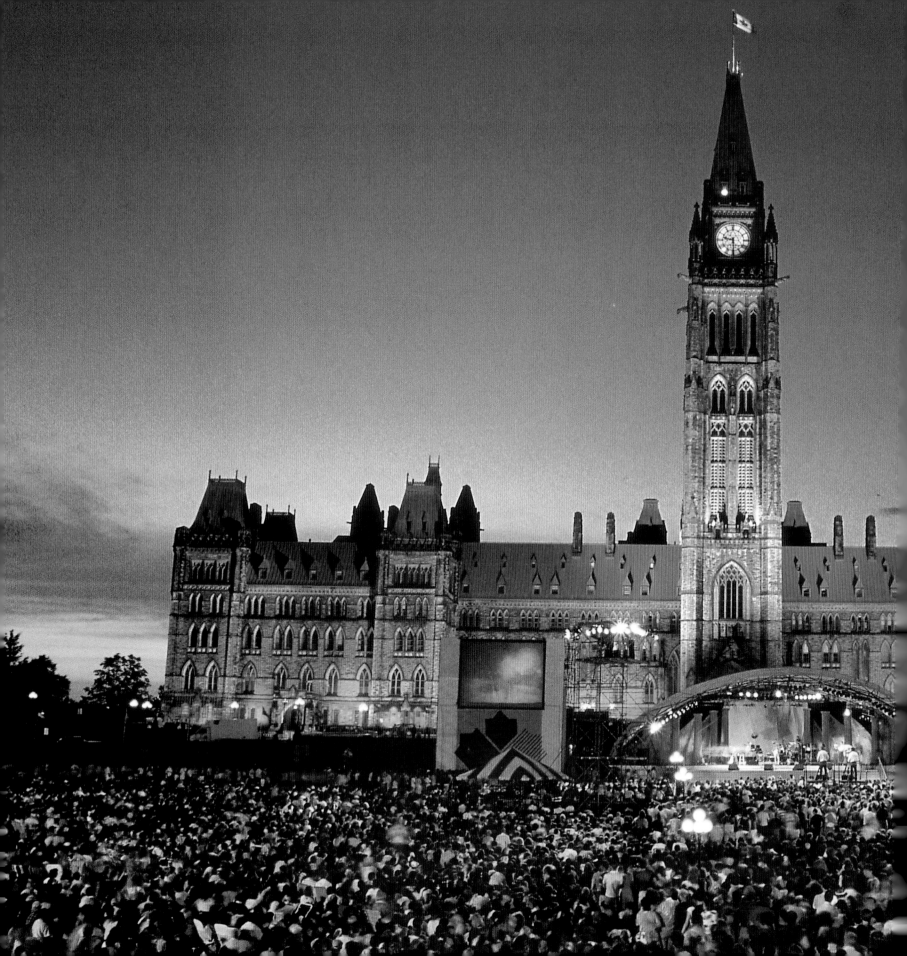

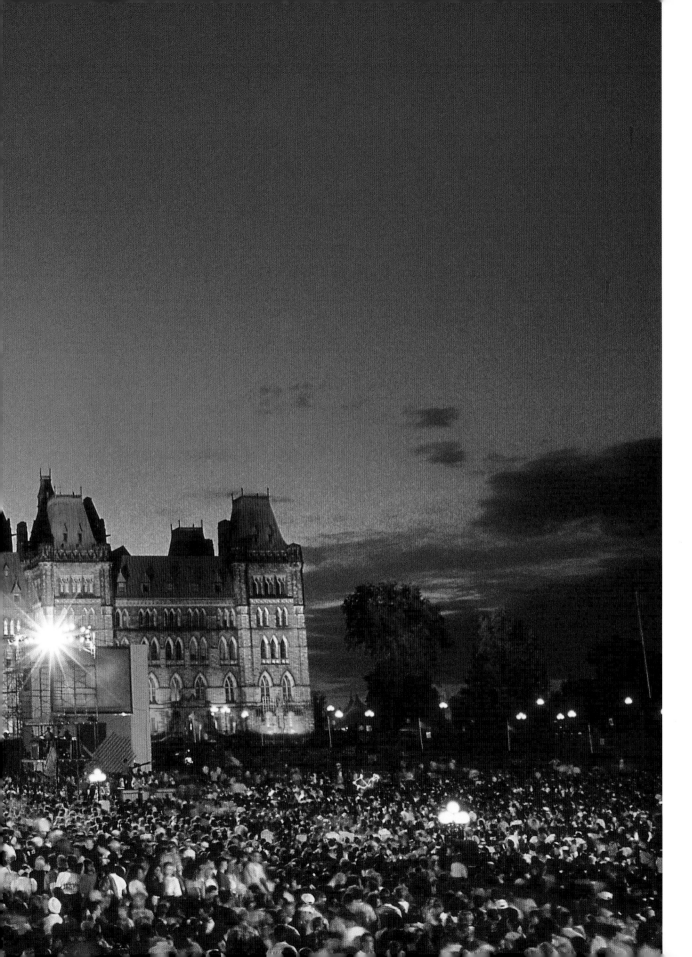

From the changing of the guards in the morning to music and fireworks well after dark, Parliament Hill is the centre of Canada Day activities, held July 1.

41

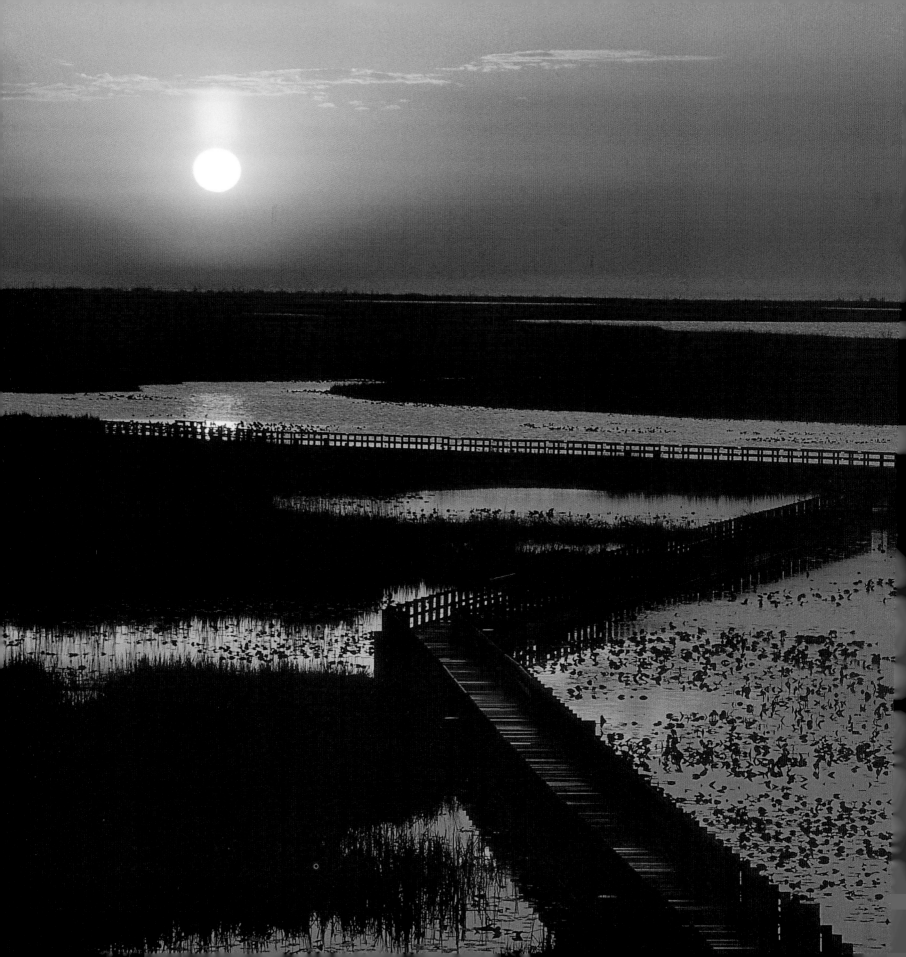

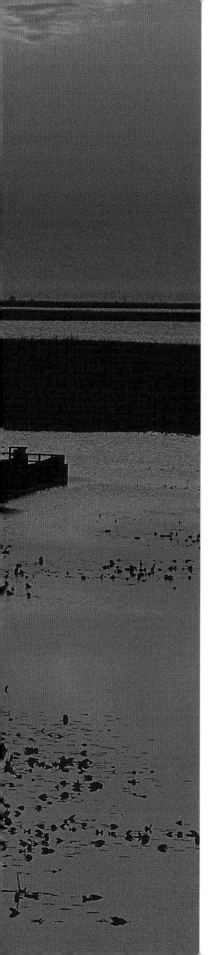

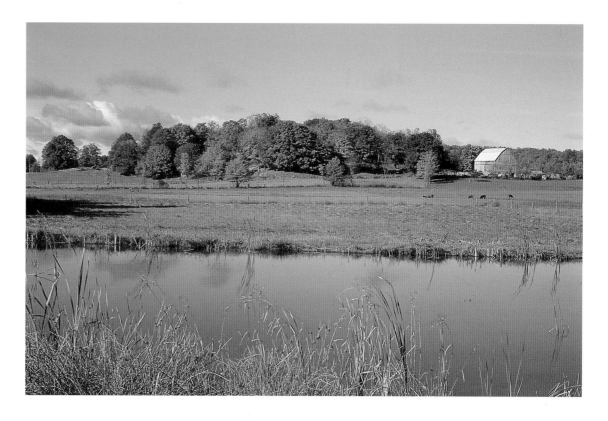

Ontario produces an annual wheat crop valued at more than $100 million, making the province Canada's fourth-largest producer. Ontario leads the country in the production of poultry, dairy products, vegetables, and eggs.

Canada's southernmost tip, Point Pelee, Ontario, is at the same latitude as northern California. Thousands of birds stop here on their annual migrations, and they are joined each fall by flights of monarch butterflies.

OVERLEAF –
Known as the crown jewel of Ontario's provincial park system, 48,500-hectare Killarney Provincial Park provides inspiring scenery at the western edge of Georgian Bay. The park is accessible only by foot or canoe.

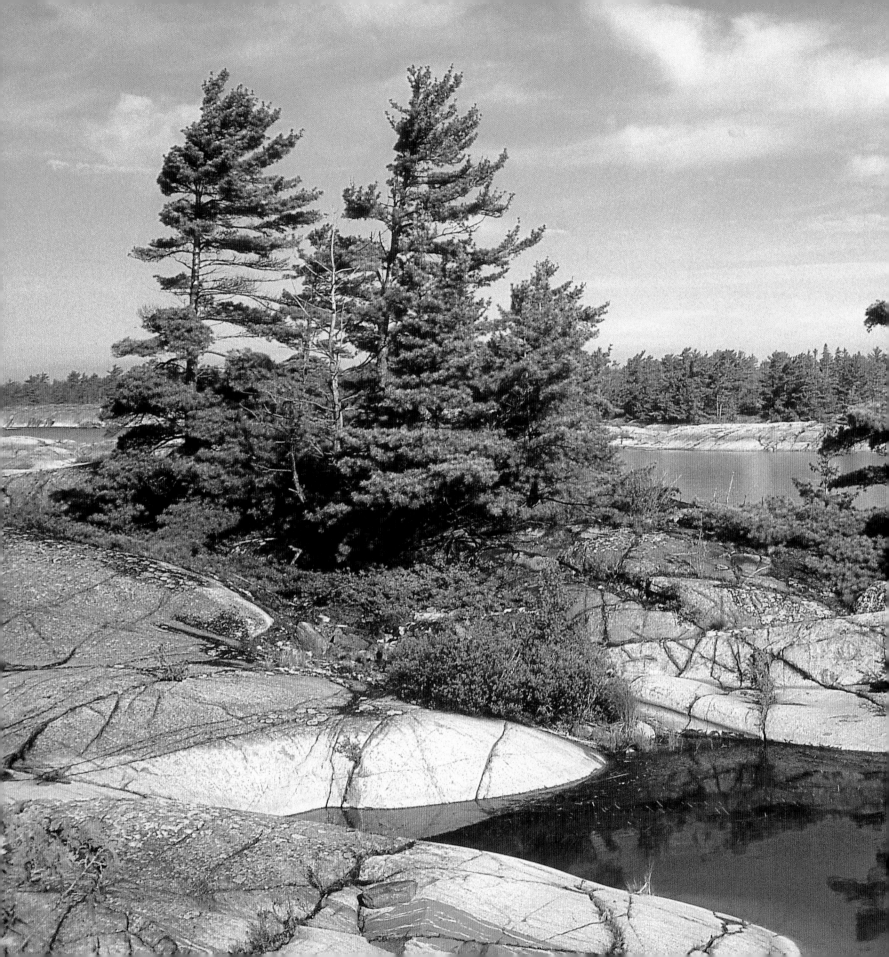

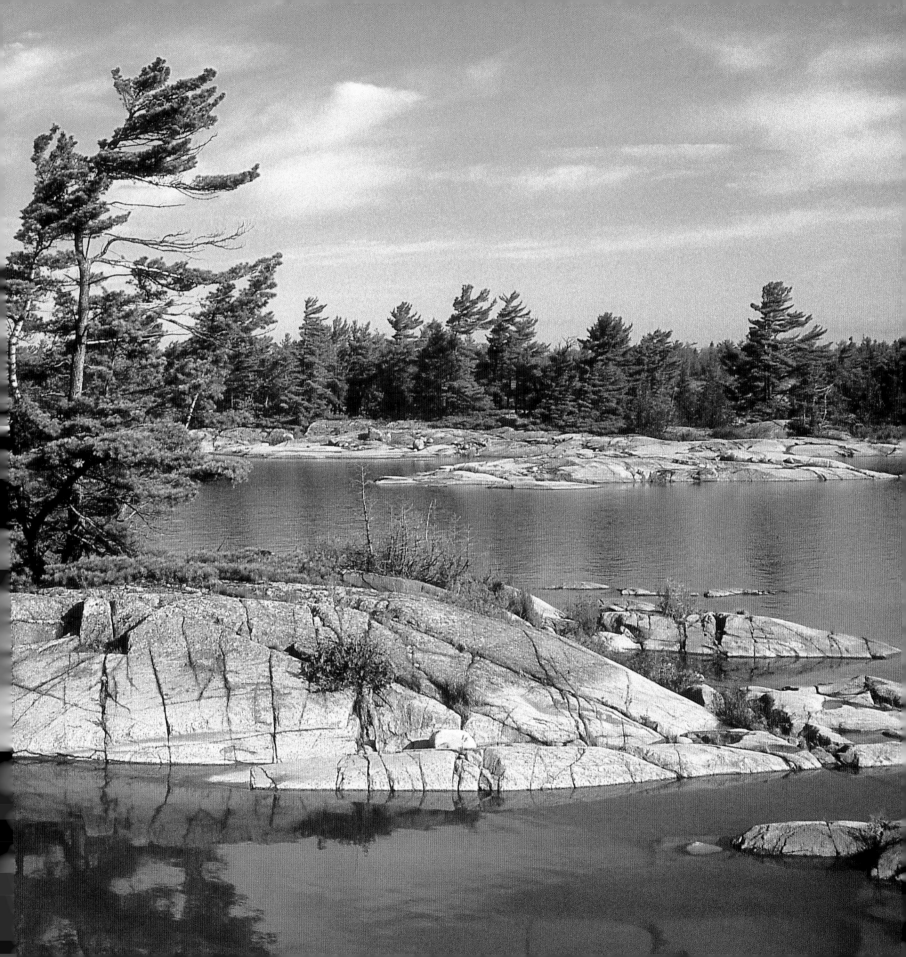

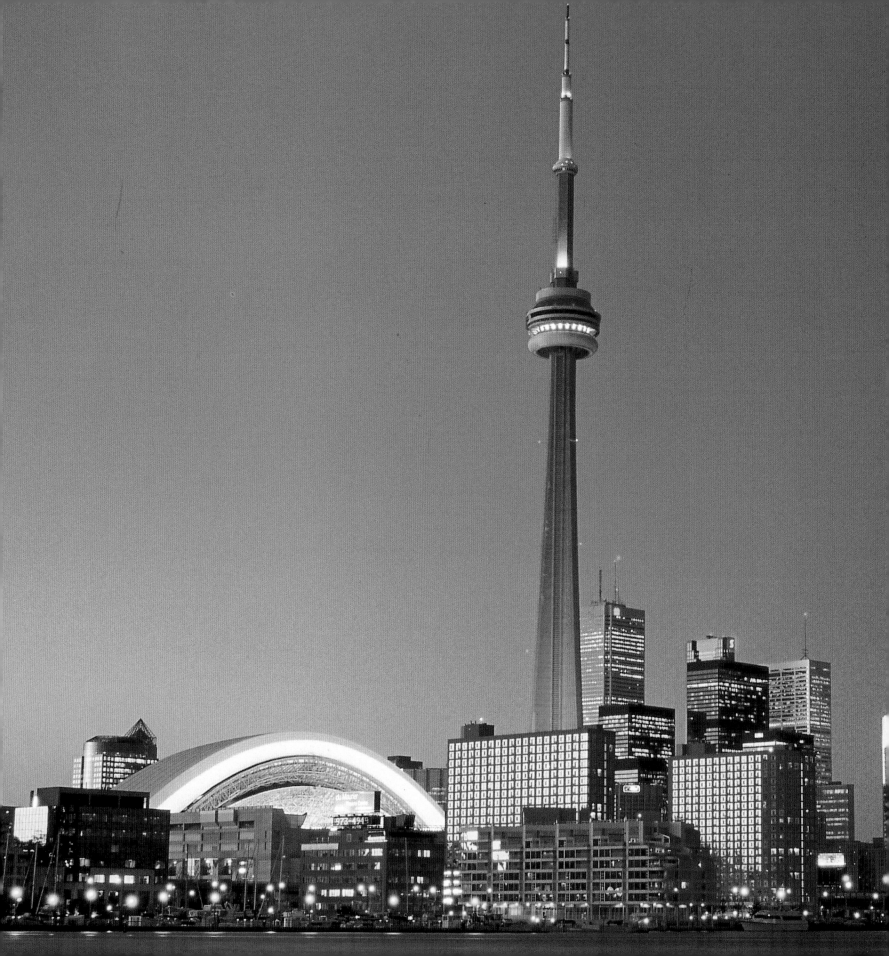

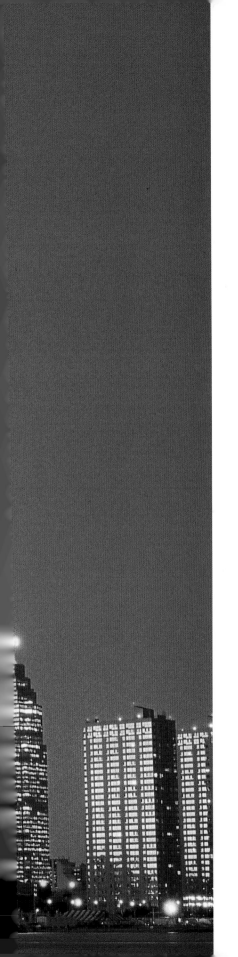

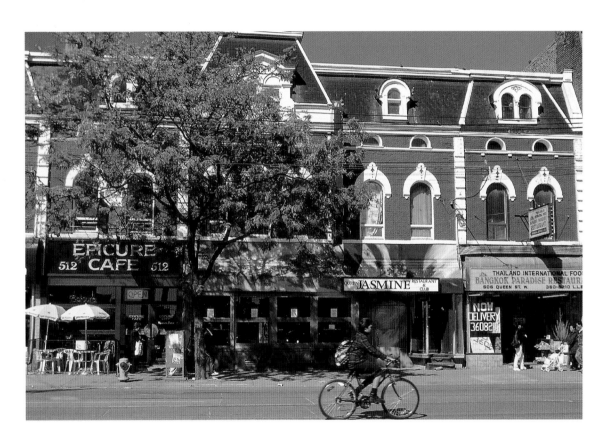

Queen Street West is one of the many small neighbourhoods that make Toronto unique. The area combines historic storefronts with cafés, private art galleries, and specialty shops, including the largest comic-book store in North America. The Ontario College of Art is located nearby.

Toronto, Ontario's capital city, is a thriving blend of high finance, modern architecture, cosmopolitan neighbourhoods, and cultural venues. Rising above the skyline, the 553-metre CN Tower is the tallest free-standing structure in the world.

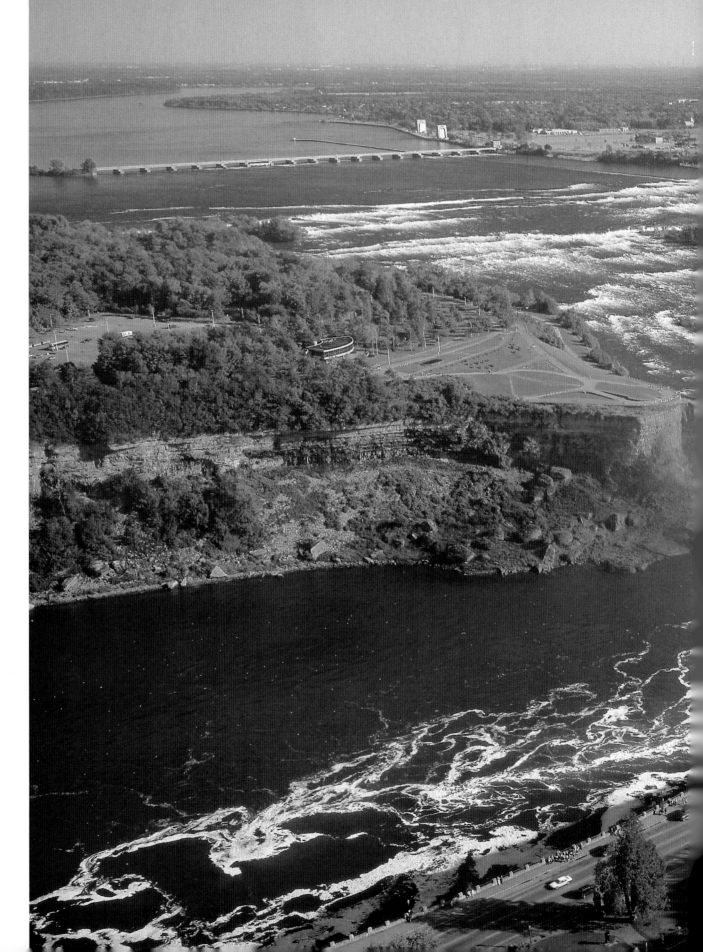

The seventh natural wonder of the world, Niagara Falls attracts more than 12 million visitors annually. Millions of litres of water cascade over the falls—so much that the cliff edge beneath the river erodes at a rate of three centimetres per year.

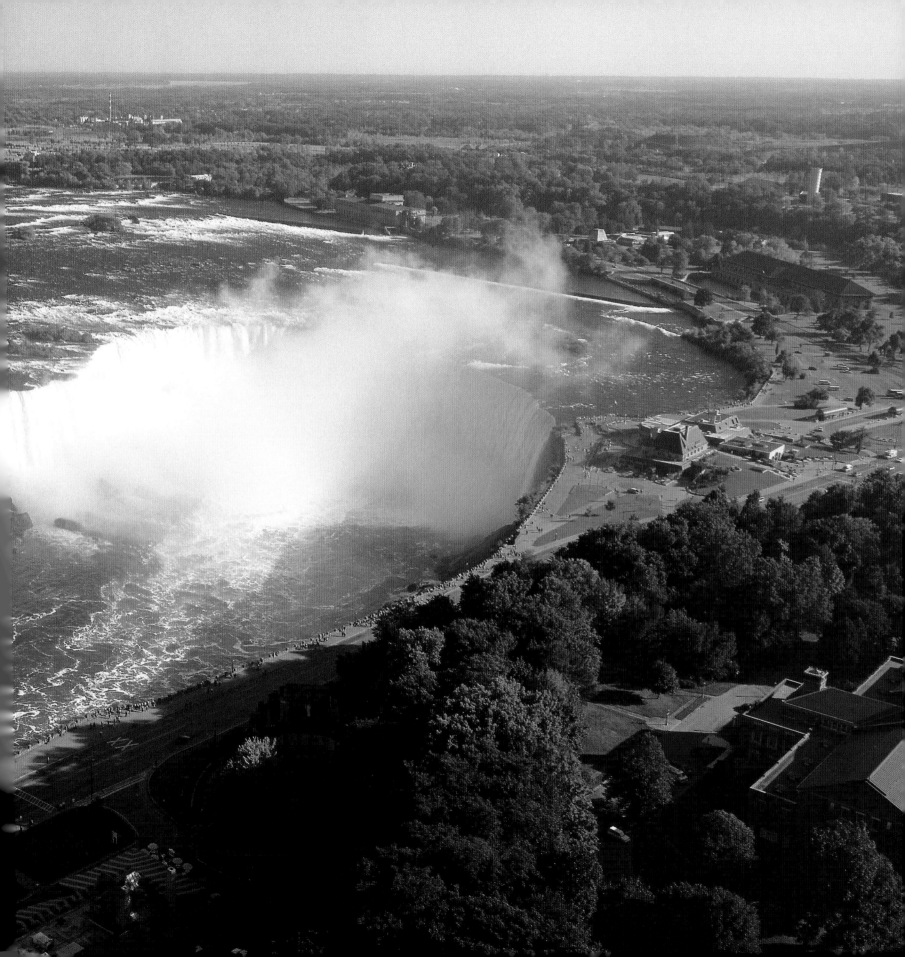

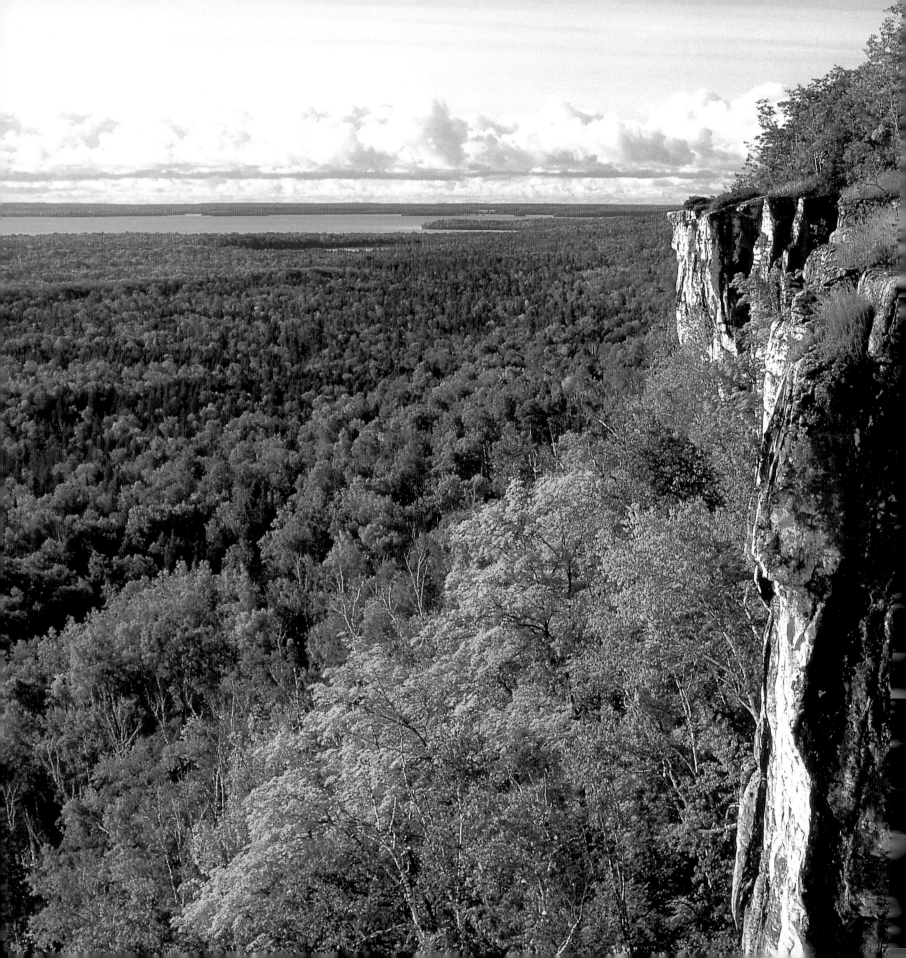

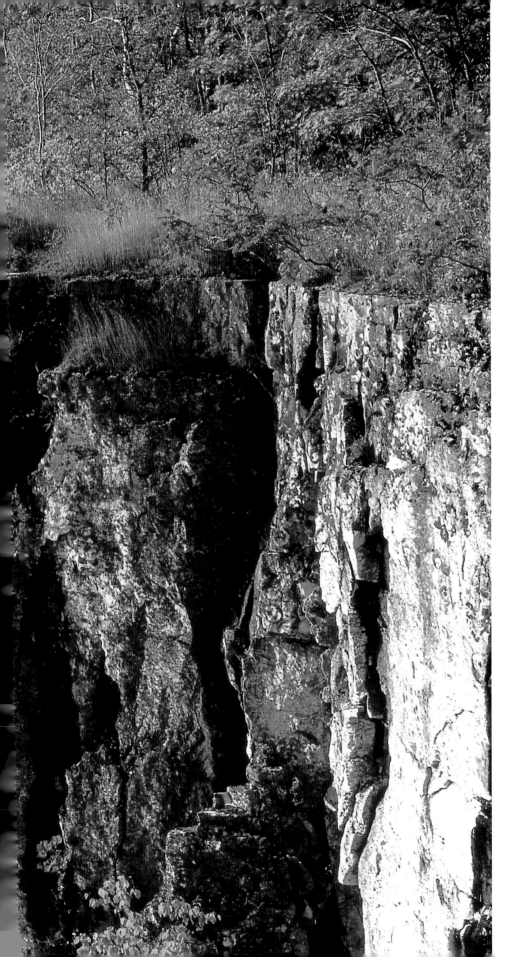

According to a First Nations legend, the Great Spirit first created life on Ontario's Manitoulin Island. Today it's a favourite with outdoor enthusiasts who hike the Cup and Saucer Trail past thick forest and intriguing rock formations.

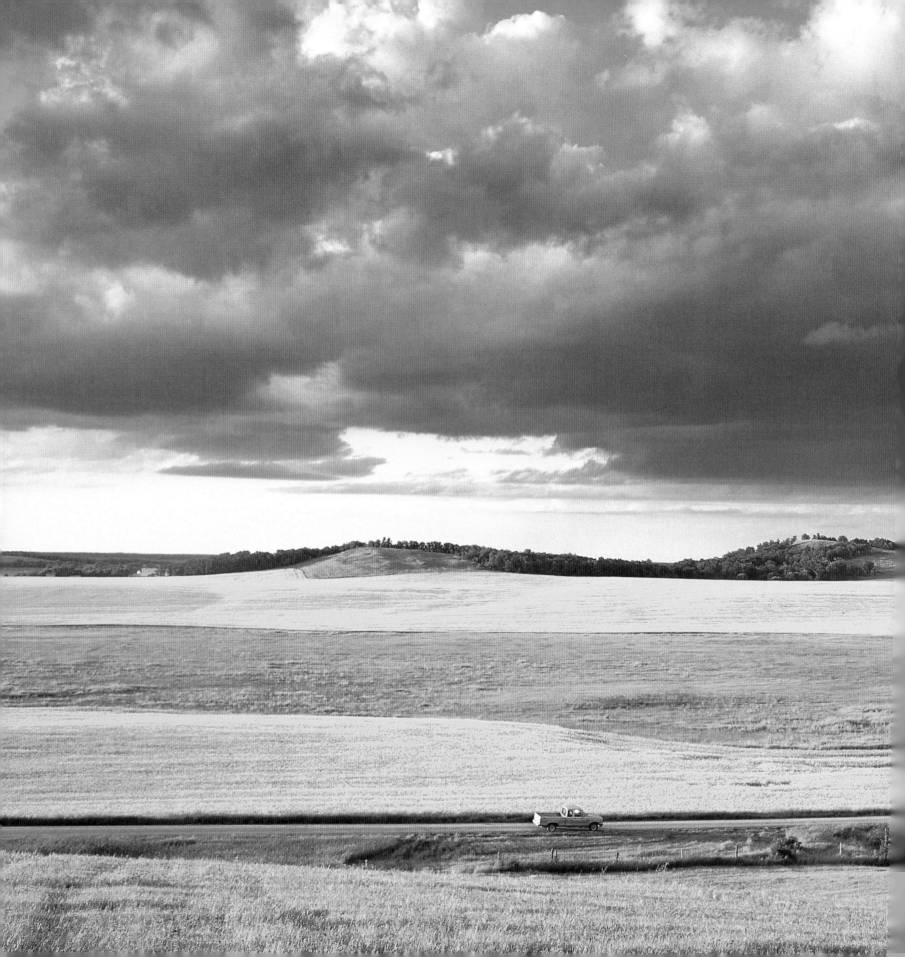

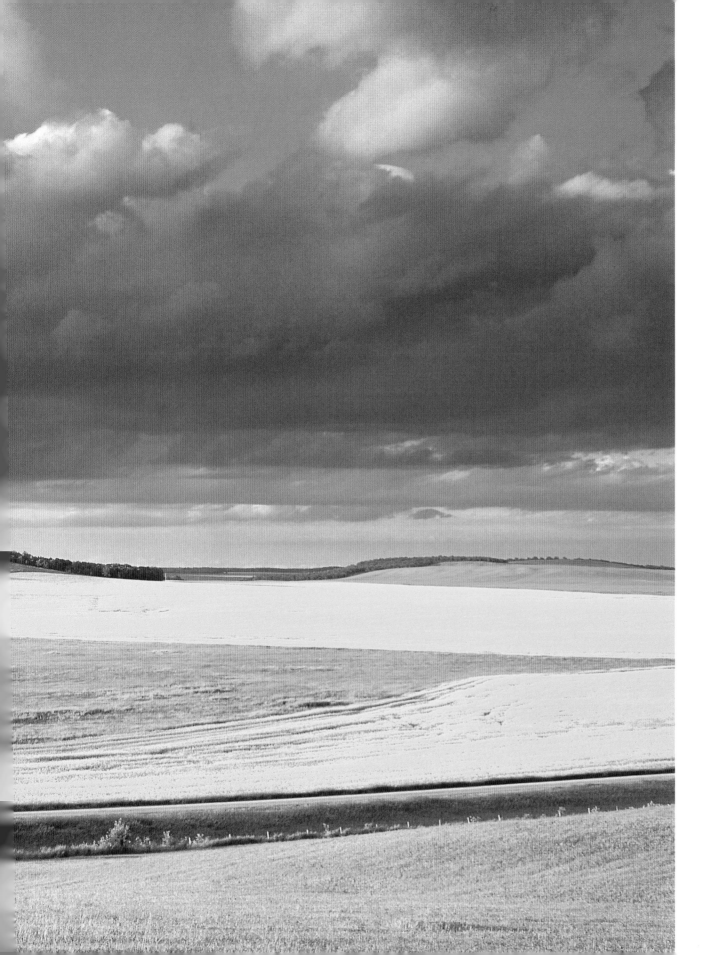

Europeans were lured to Manitoba by the fur trade, exploring and trading for the Hudson's Bay Company and the North West Company. Agriculture began to take over as an economic staple in the 1800s, when settlers gathered in the Red River Colony and present-day Winnipeg. More than 25,000 farms now checker the province.

Southern Manitoba was covered by huge glacial lakes at the end of the last ice age. This land near Dufresne was under more than 80 metres of water. The lakes left behind rich soil, responsible for today's grain crops.

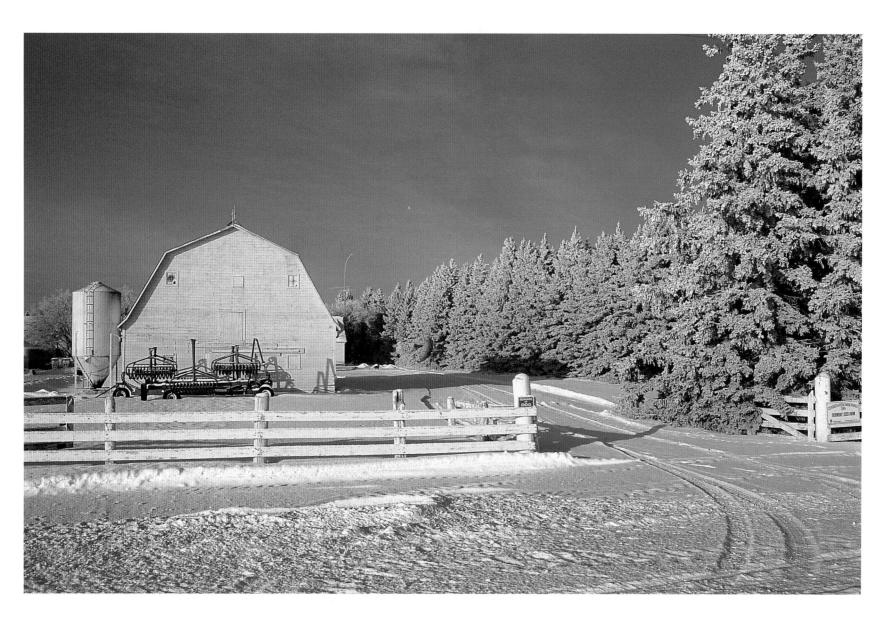

Manitoba's first frost usually arrives in September and the last is not until May. In midwinter, the average temperature drops to almost -20° Celsius.

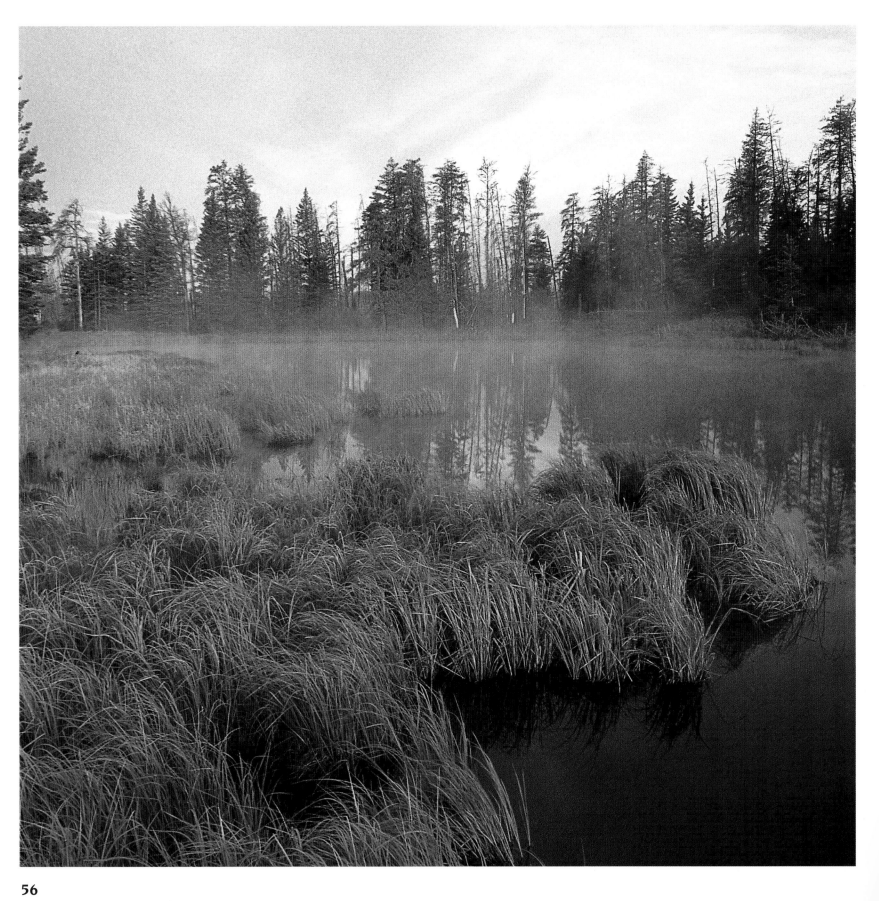

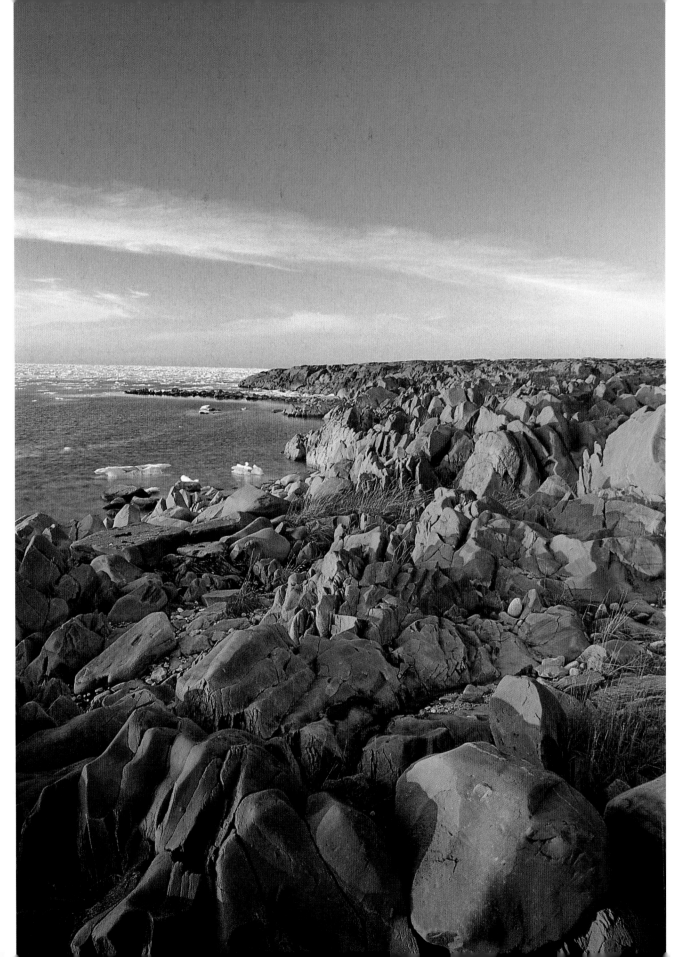

The land along the Hudson Bay coast in Manitoba, home to polar bears and arctic wildflowers, is locked in ice for eight months of the year. Even in summer, huge chunks of ice float near the shore.

FACING PAGE –
Riding Mountain National Park, northwest of Winnipeg, is home to the world's largest black bears. The park has been named a Biosphere Reserve by UNESCO and serves as an international model of how humans and nature can co-exist.

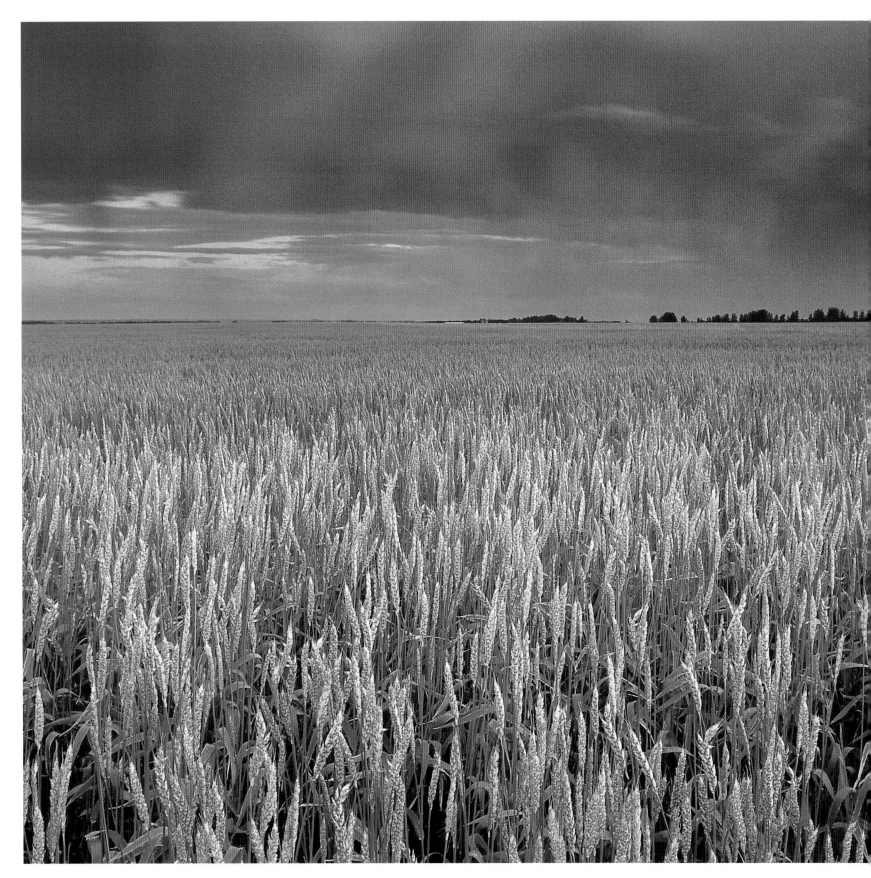

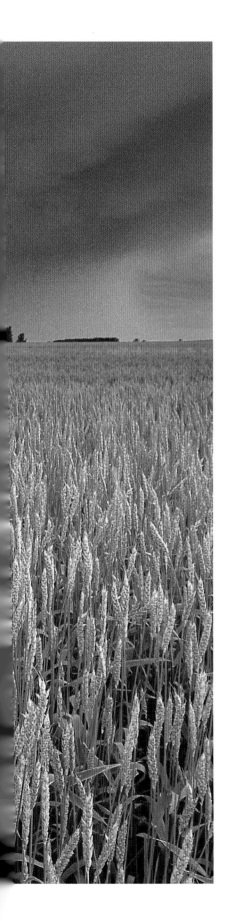

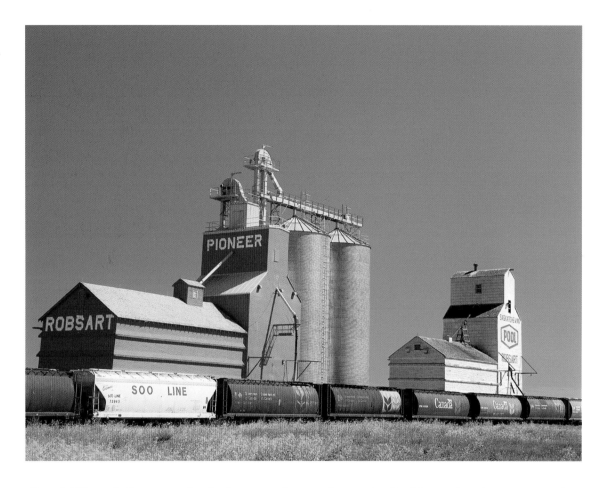

Two billion dollars worth of wheat each year is stockpiled in grain elevators such as these ones near Robsart, Saskatchewan. It is then transported by train to port cities and shipped to countries around the world, including Italy, Iran, Algeria, France, and Russia.

Wheat, the staple of Saskatchewan's economy, is not indigenous to North America. It was brought by some of the first North American settlers. The first wheat was planted in western Canada in 1754 in the Carrot River Valley.

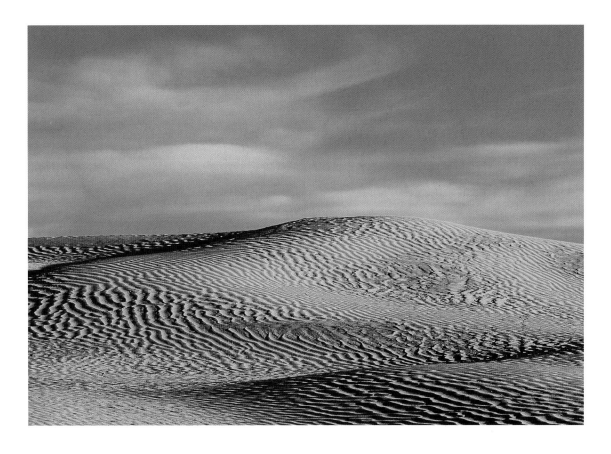

The Great Sand Hills of Saskatchewan, swept bare by the wind, span 1,900 square kilometres between Maple Creek, Leader, and Webb. Deer, grouse, coyotes, and owls inhabit the dunes.

Saskatchewan's Prince Albert National Park encompasses hundreds of tiny lakes and several large ones, including Waskesiu Lake. Trails throughout the park are ideal for hiking, cross-country skiing, or cycling.

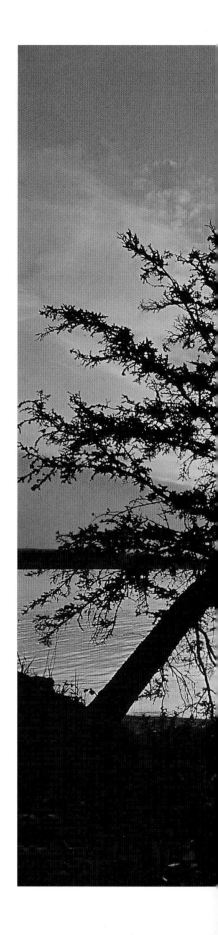

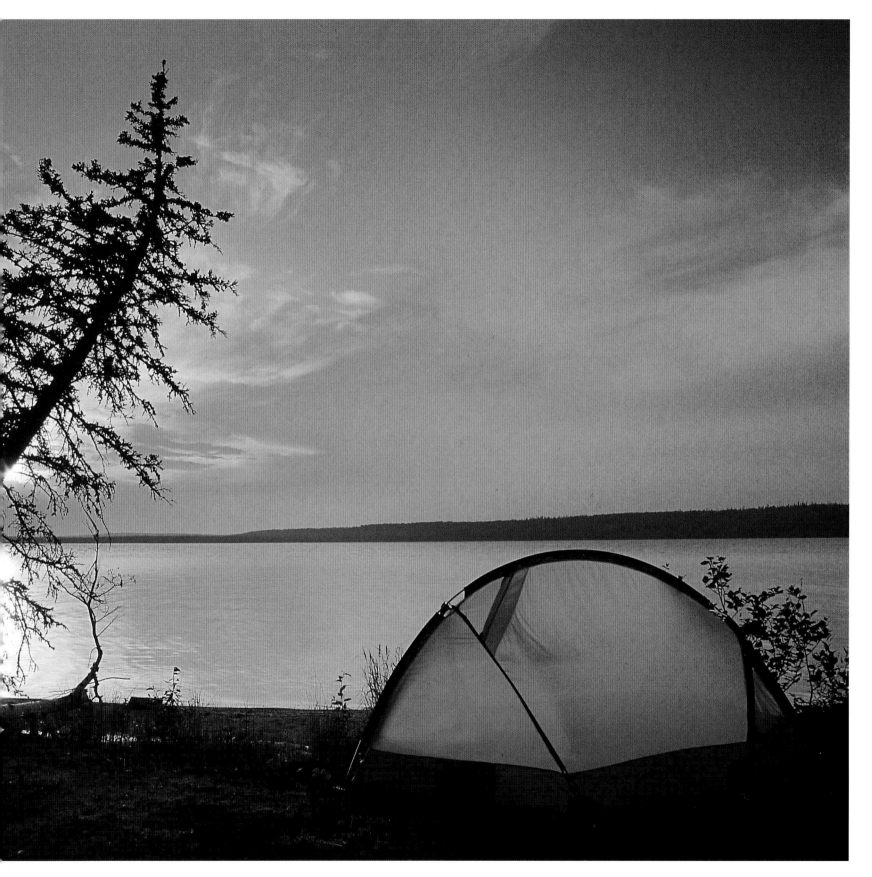

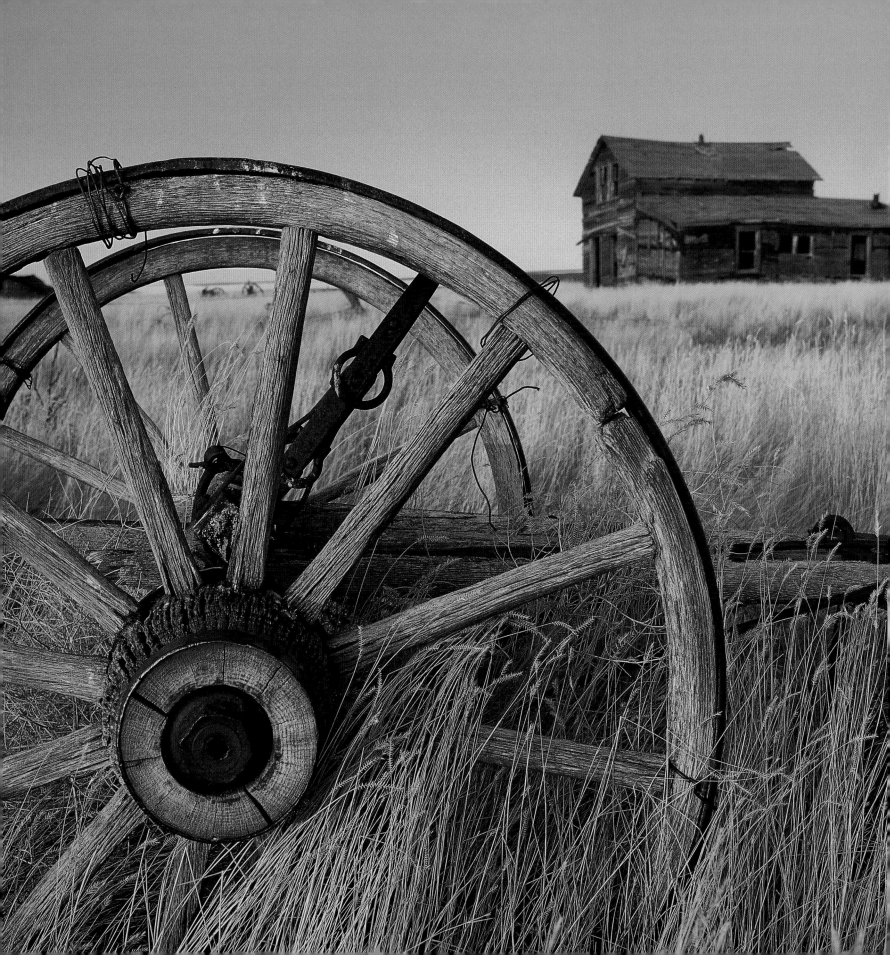

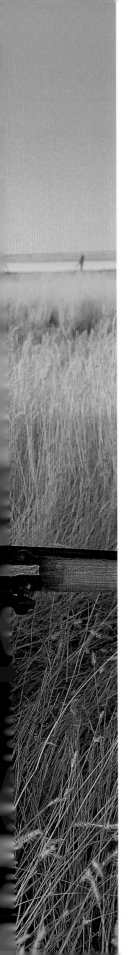

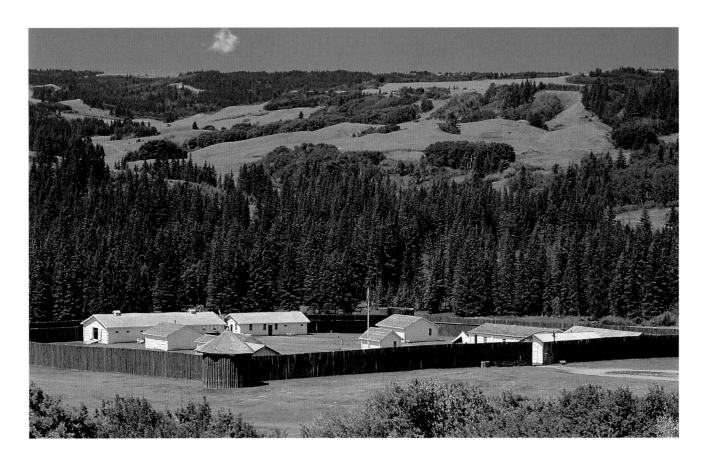

Fort Walsh was established by the North-West Mounted Police in response to unrestricted whiskey and fur trading in the late 1800s. In 1873, wolf hunters killed 20 natives near here in what is now known as the Cypress Hills Massacre.

Picturesque farmland surrounds Ponteix in southern Saskatchewan. The town was founded by Father Albert Royer, a Roman Catholic missionary, and named after his parish in France.

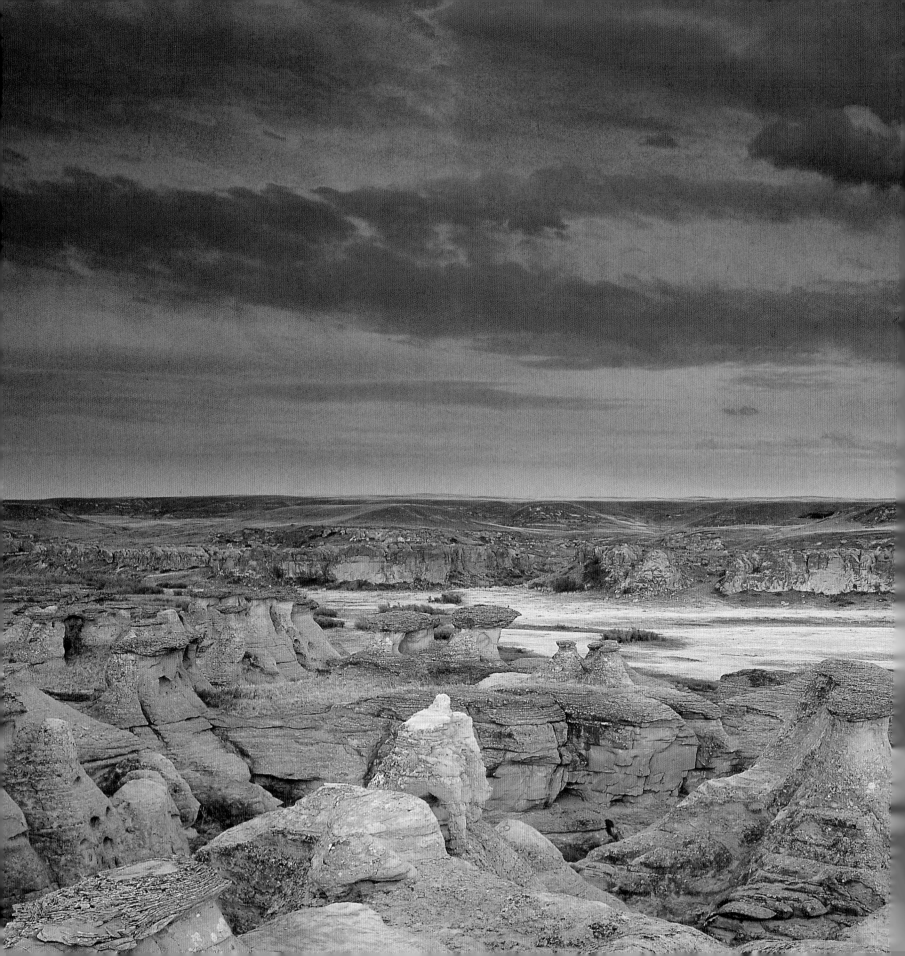

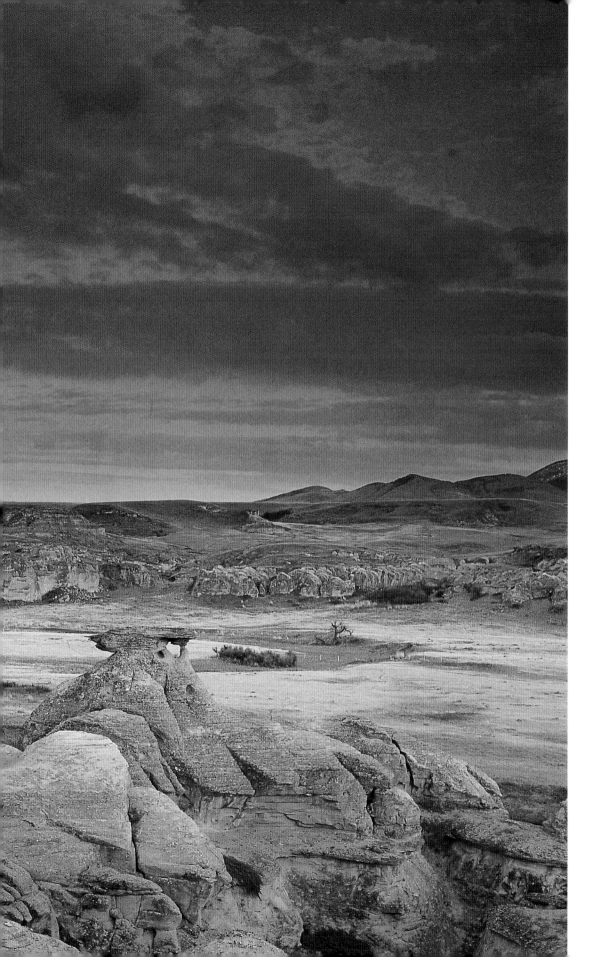

The hoodoos at Alberta's Writing-on-Stone Provincial Park were formed by erosion. A hard cap tops each hoodoo, protecting it from the wind and rain that abraded the surrounding stone. Eventually, the caps are also worn away and the hoodoos diminish in size.

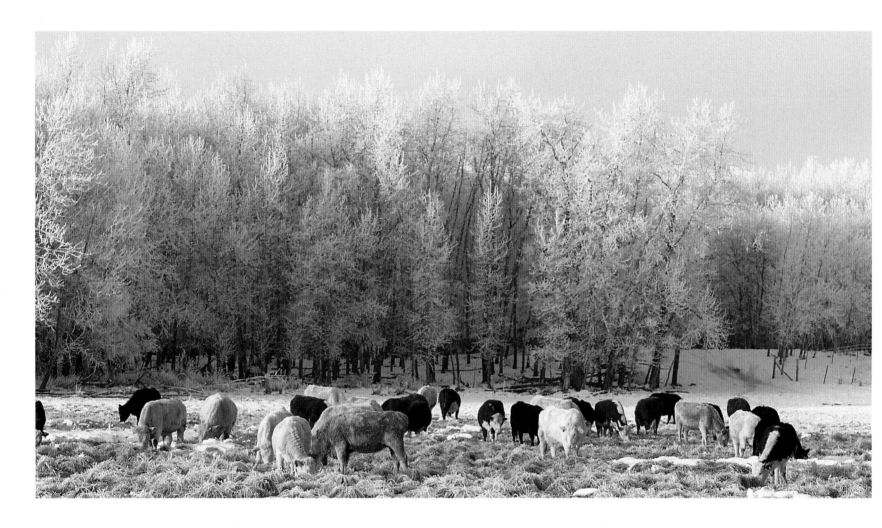

Alberta's agricultural communities give the impression of an old-fashioned lifestyle, but Alberta has often been one of Canada's most progressive regions. In 1916, for example, it became one of the first provinces to allow women to vote.

Albertans don't plant canola just for its eyecatching colour; annual export sales account for almost $700 million. The harvest from this field near Leduc, Alberta, will find its way into a wide range of products, from cosmetics to medicine.

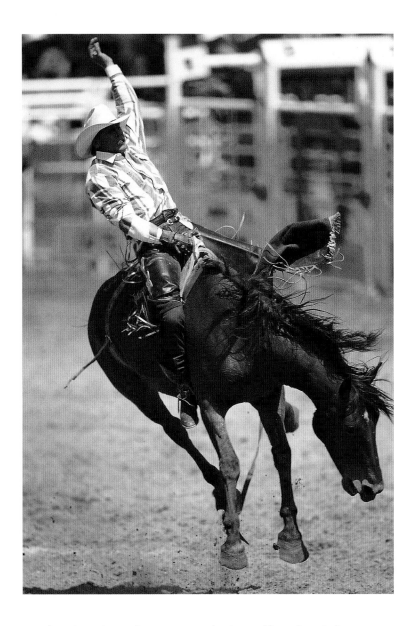

Professional cowboys strut their stuff at the Calgary Stampede, the largest rodeo on earth. The stampede attracts more than one million visitors each July to the 38-hectare Stampede Park. About 1,700 volunteers and 1,500 employees look after the crowds and keep events on schedule.

When the Calgary Flames are in town, spectators pack the Olympic Saddledome. Built for the 1988 Winter Olympics, the distinctive arena seats 20,000 people.

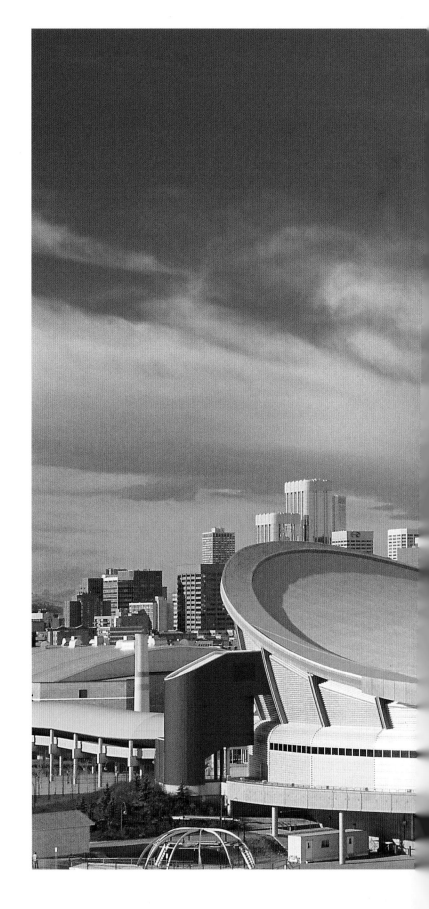

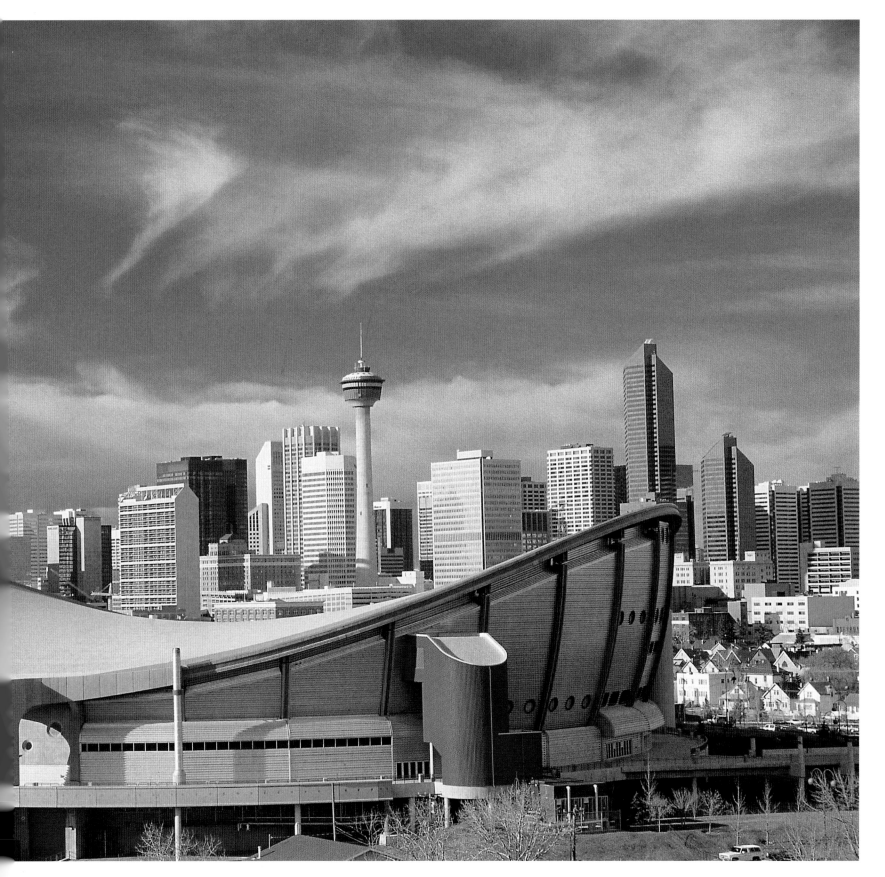

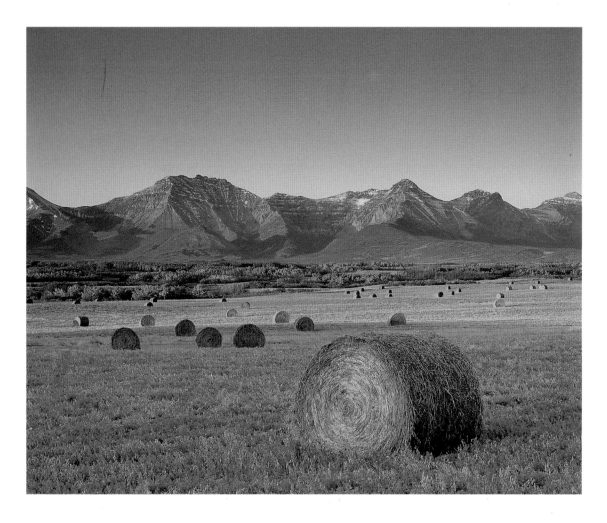

Although Alberta was settled by farmers, only 20 percent of the population continues to live in rural areas. The oil and gas industry now competes with agriculture as the basis of the province's economy.

Along with Banff, Yoho, and Kootenay national parks, Alberta's Jasper National Park is part of the Rocky Mountain World Heritage Site. Together, these parks protect 69 mammal species and provide the range needed by large animals such as grizzly bears. Only one-tenth of the park is valley bottoms. The rest is pure height—jagged cliffs, glaciers, peaks, and alpine meadows.

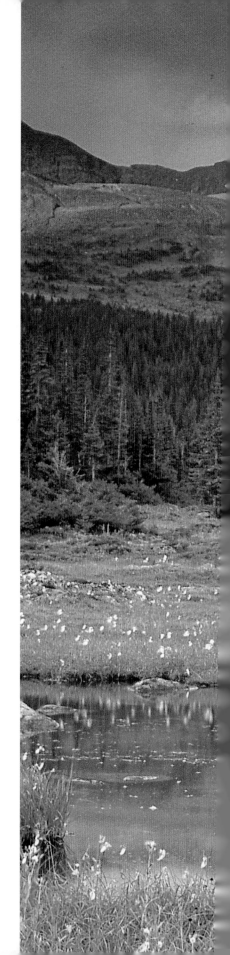

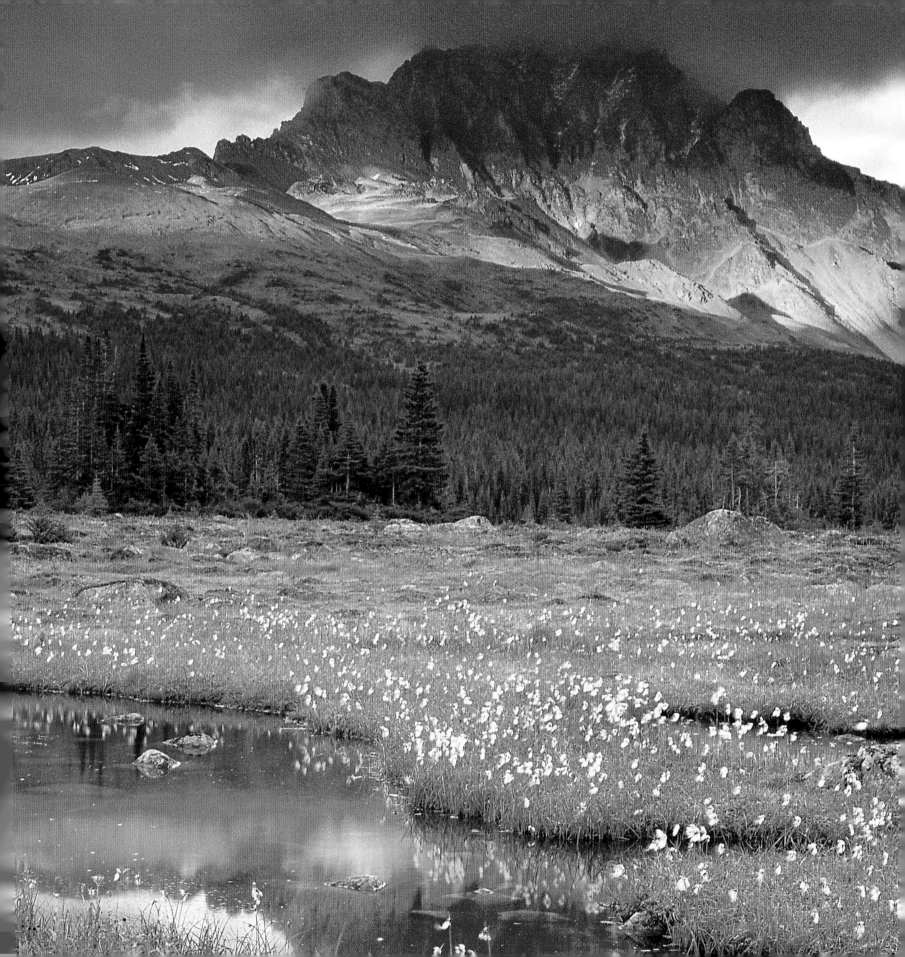

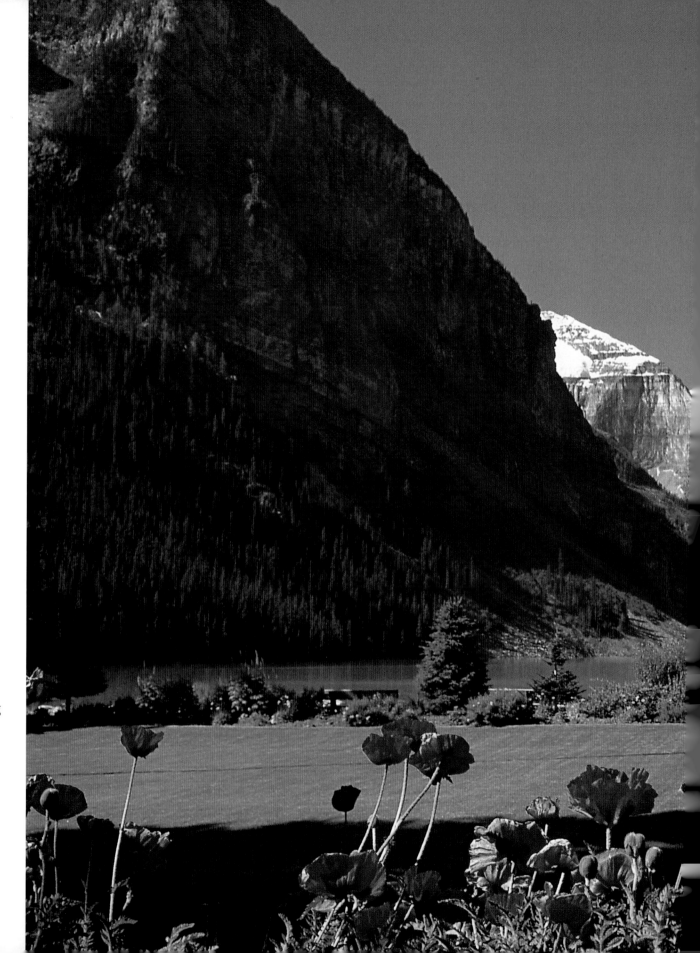

Each summer, Banff National Park hosts 50,000 tourists a day. One of the park's most popular attractions is Lake Louise, a stunning 2.4-kilometre-long lake fed by Victoria Glacier, visible in the distance.

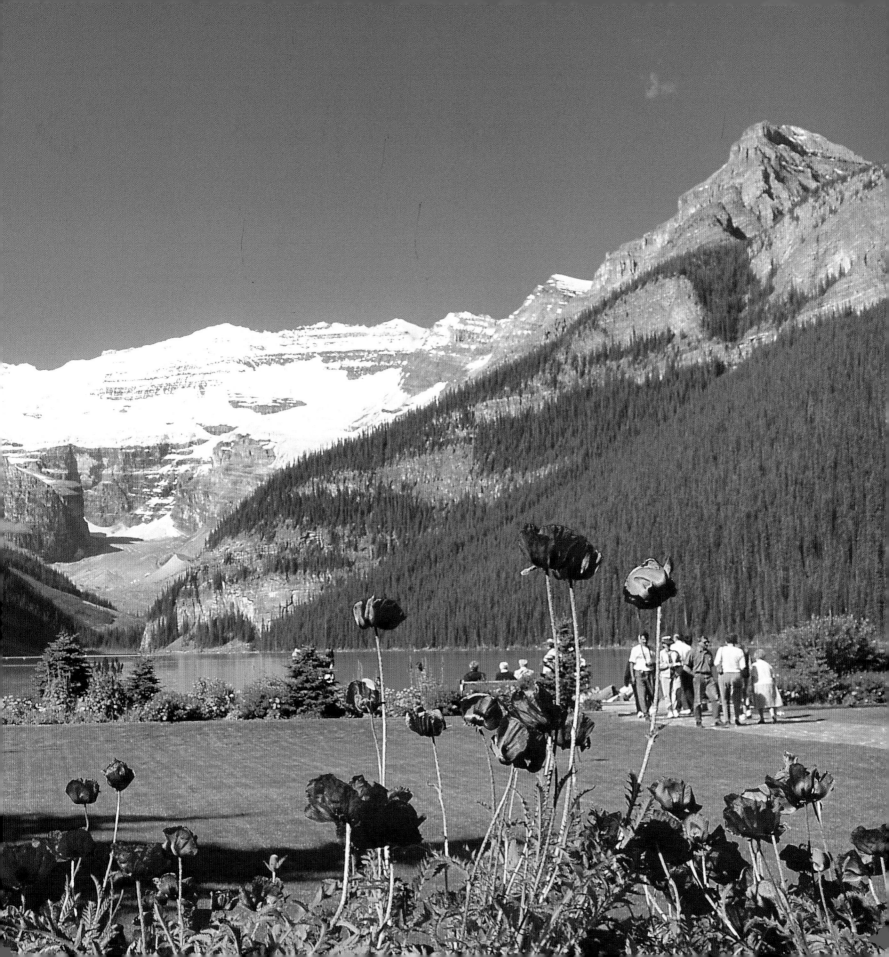

Lake O'Hara is just part of the stunning scenery that earned British Columbia's Yoho National Park its name. *Yoho* means "wonder" or "awe" in the language of the Kootenai peoples. The cabin at Lake O'Hara is a popular base for cross-country skiing in winter and hiking in summer. More than 360 kilometres of trails crisscross the park.

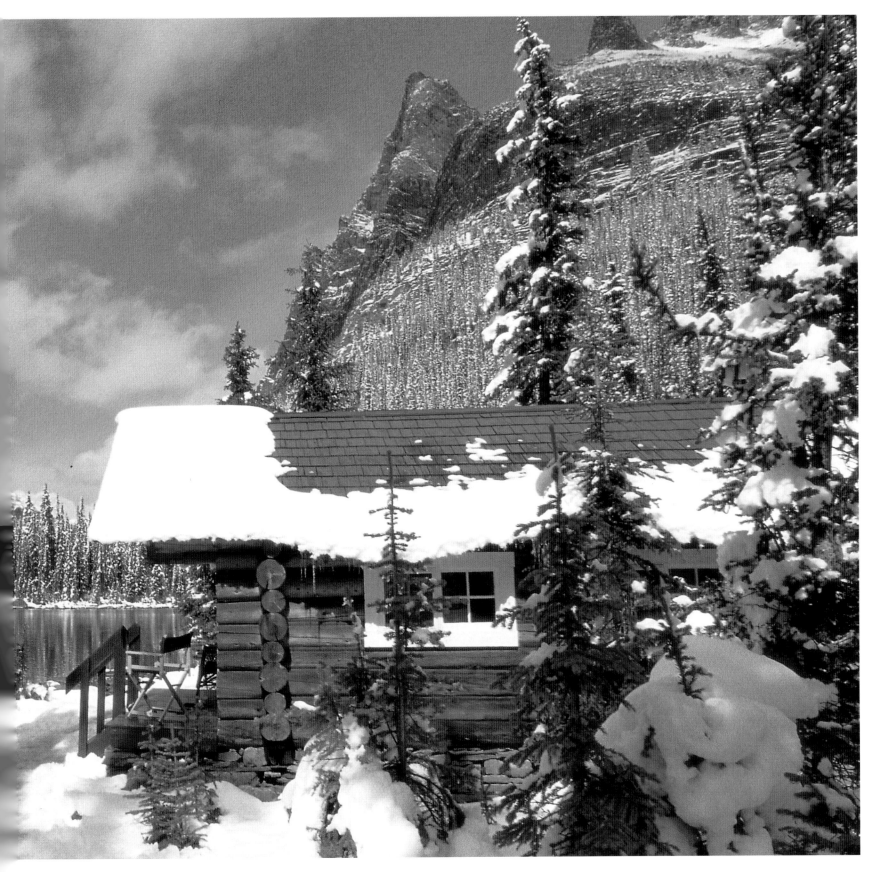

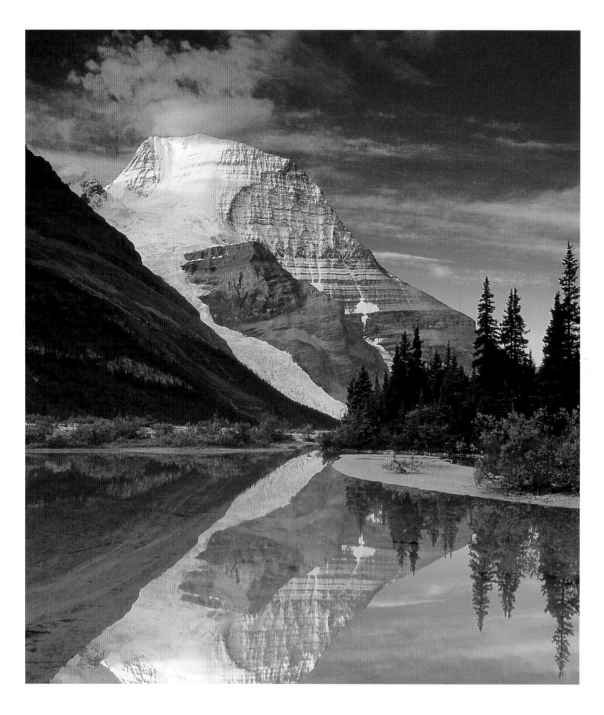

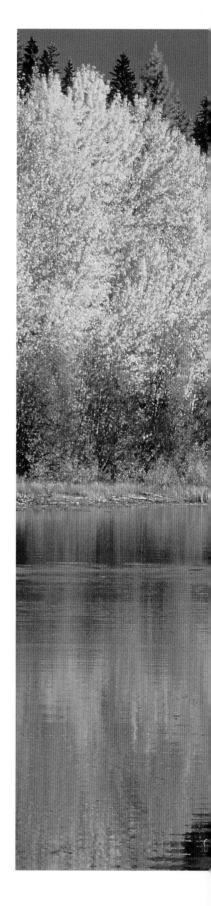

At 3,954 metres, Mount Robson is the highest peak in the Canadian Rockies. Its summit, almost always obscured by cloud, was first conquered in 1913. It is still accessible to only the most dedicated mountaineers.

British Columbia's Cariboo-Chilcotin region extends from the Pacific east to the Cariboo Mountains. Its remote wilderness regions and plentiful waterways draw backpackers and canoeists each summer.

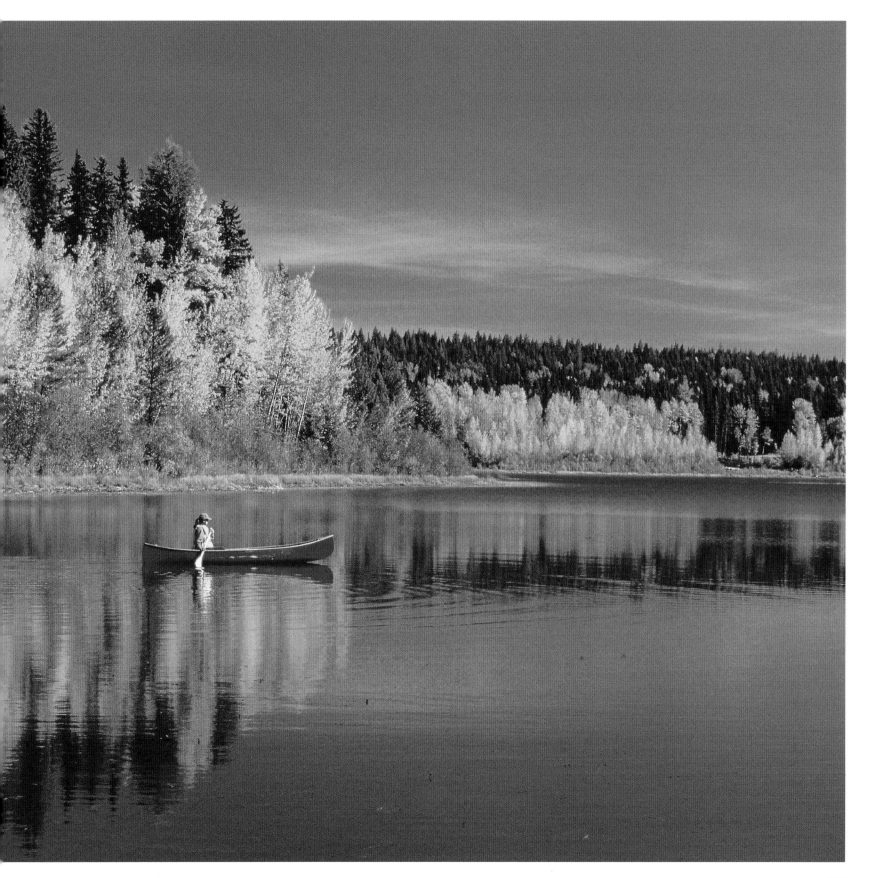

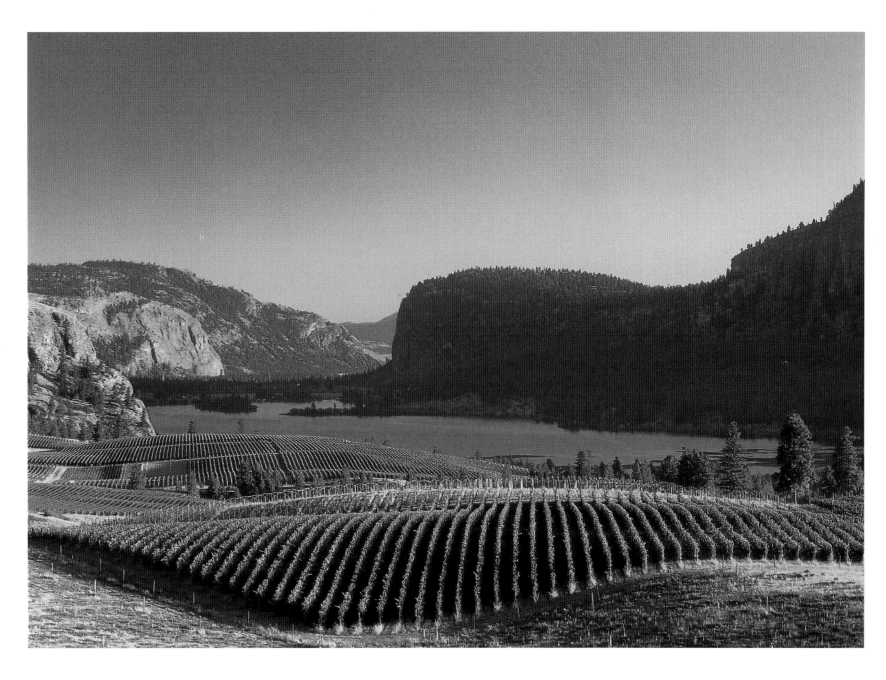

Blue Mountain Vineyards is one of many that take advantage of the Okanagan's hot, dry summers. In the background lies Vaseux Lake, a bird and wildlife sanctuary that attracts trumpeter swans and Canada geese, among other species.

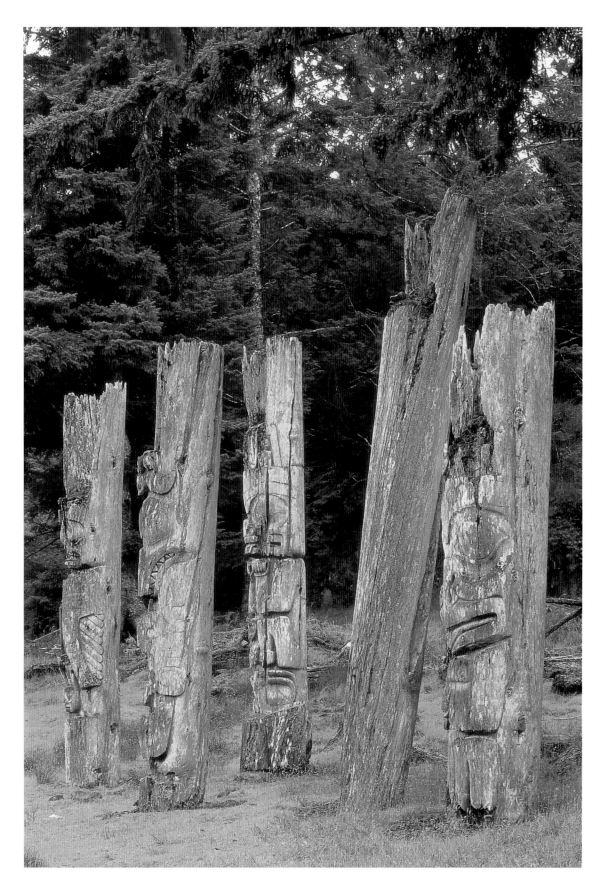

Weather-worn totems and fallen house timbers are all that remain of the once-thriving village of Ninstints, where smallpox killed most of the native population. Gwaii Haanas National Park now protects the poles, and the area has been declared a UNESCO World Heritage Site.

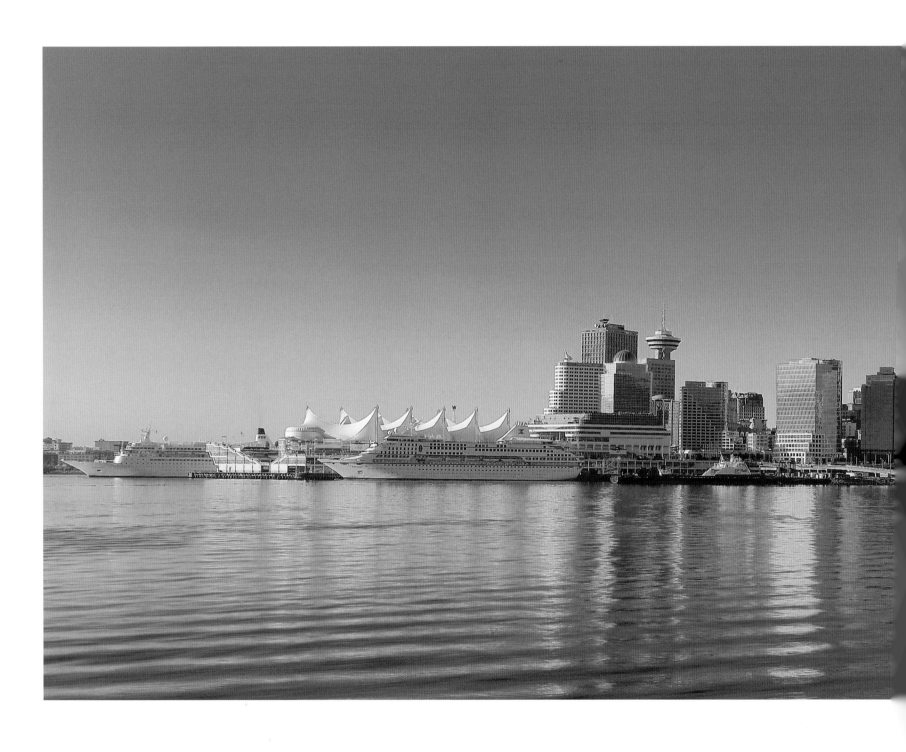

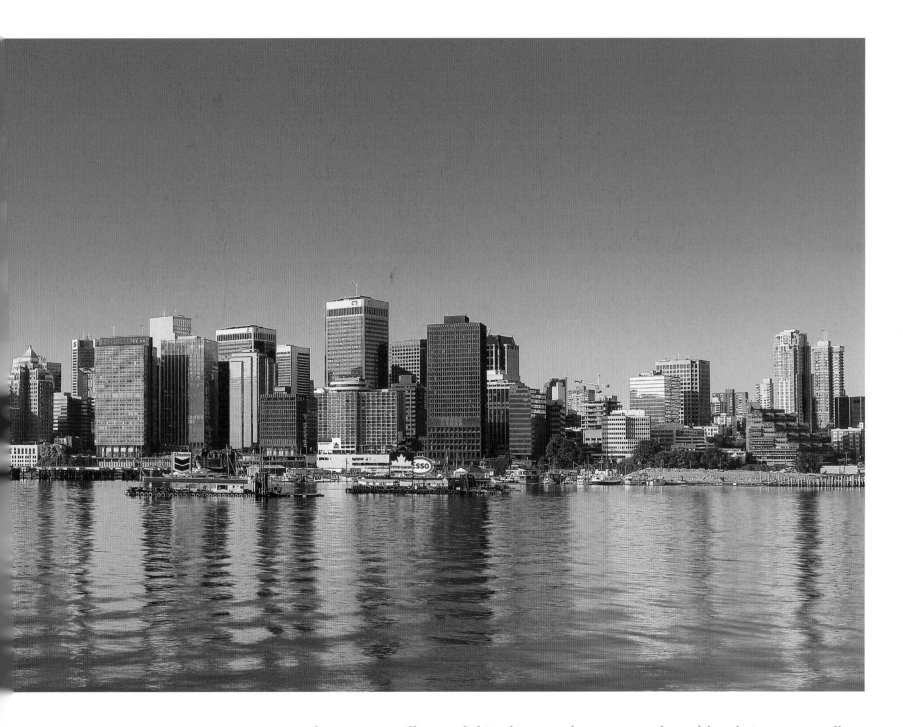

Vancouver began as a mill town, fishing base, and gateway to the gold rush. It was a small cluster of buildings along Burrard Inlet until the first transcontinental passenger train arrived in 1886 and ships began docking from every corner of the globe. Today, visitors board luxury cruise ships under the white sails of Canada Place.

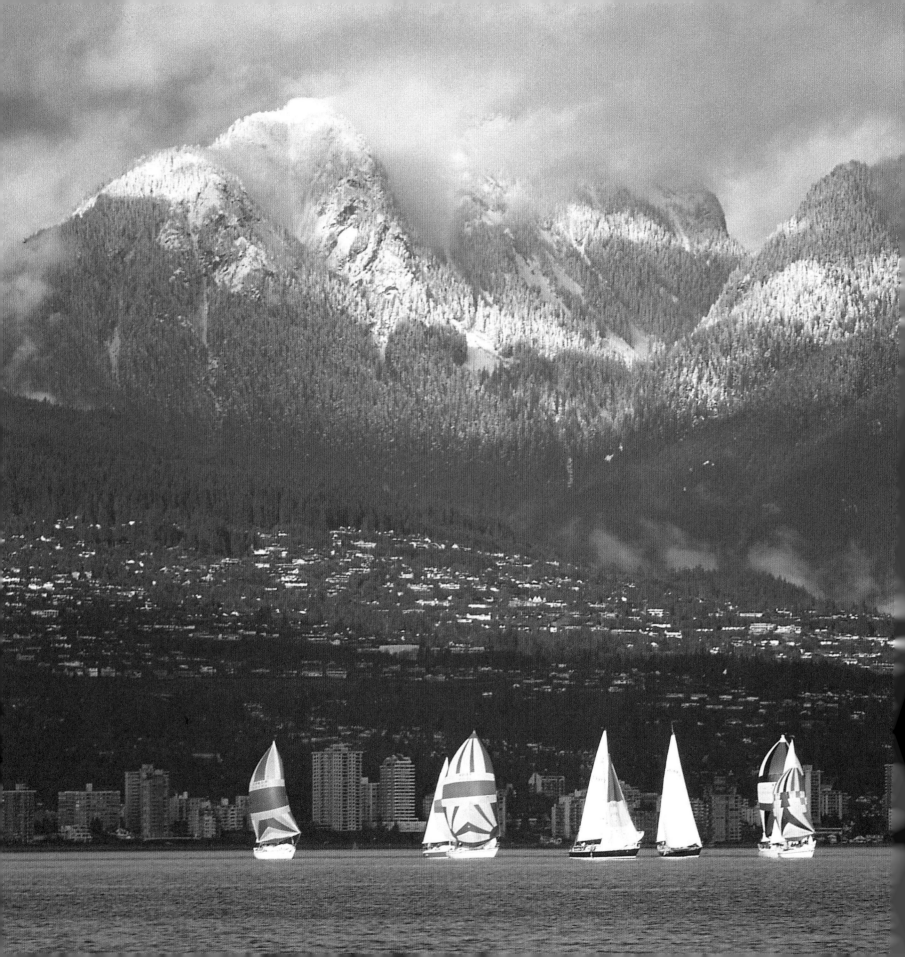

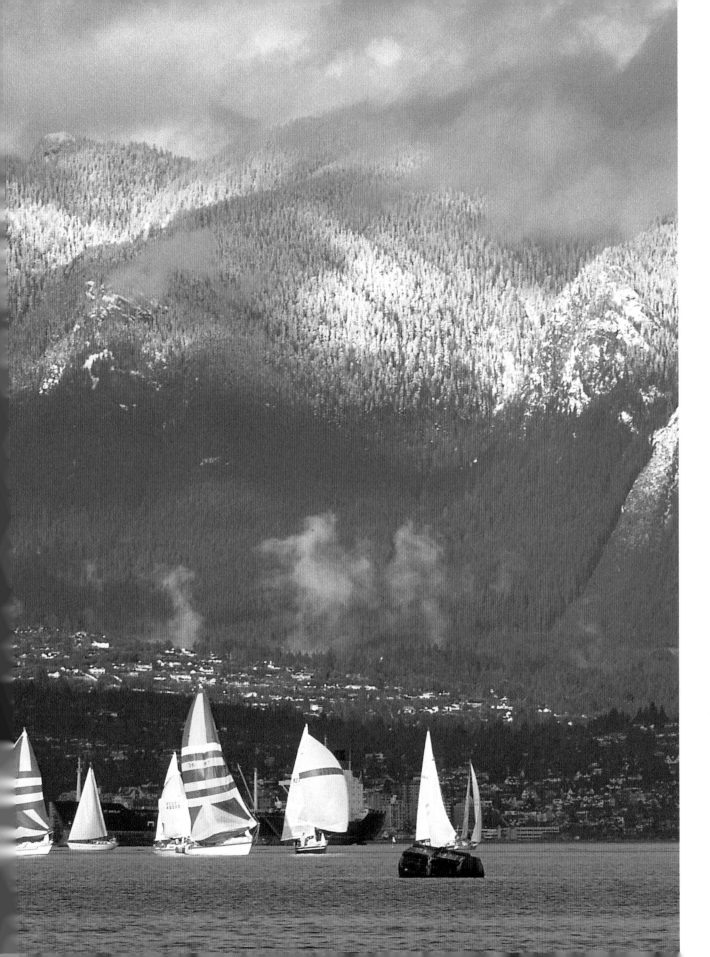

Vancouver's mild climate and coastal breezes draw hundreds of sailors to English Bay. The posh homes of West Vancouver dot the hillside to the north of the bay.

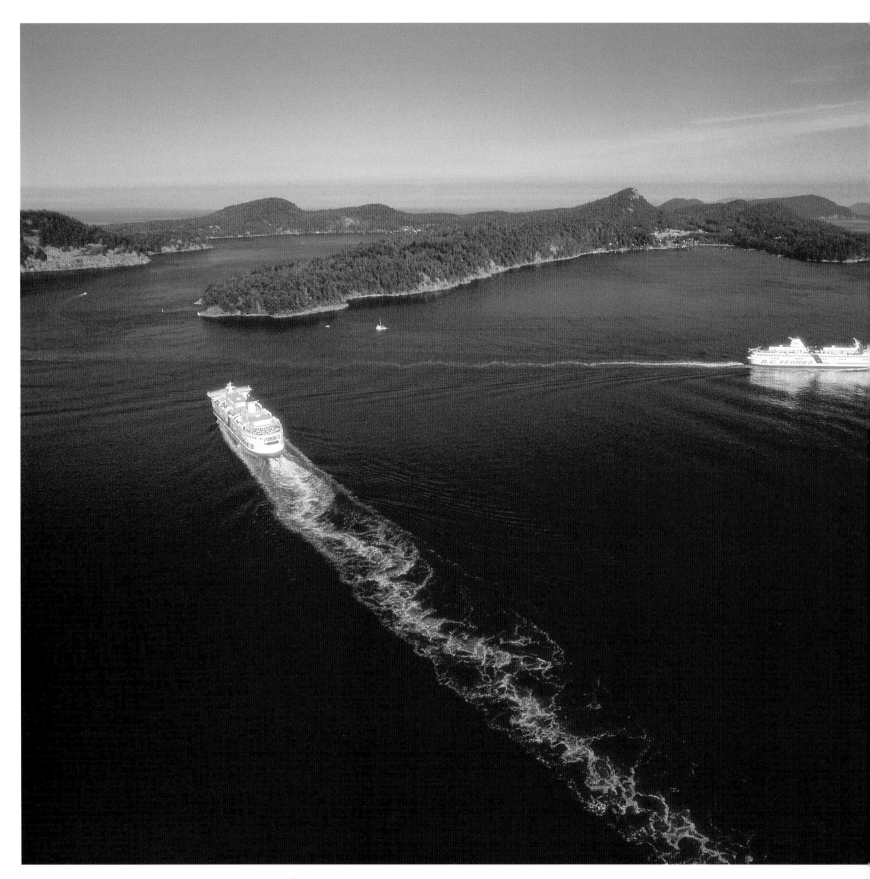

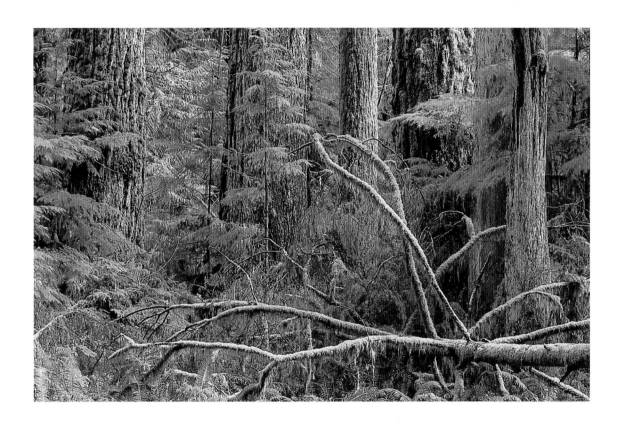

MacMillan Park's Cathedral Grove is aptly named—branches arch into the sky to screen out the sunlight. These 800-year-old trees survived a forest fire that destroyed their surroundings about 300 years ago. Now, the tallest Douglas fir is more than 75 metres high.

B.C.'s massive superferries pass in front of Mayne Island at the mouth of Active Pass. The boats run year-round between Tsawwassen, on the mainland, and Swartz Bay on Vancouver Island.

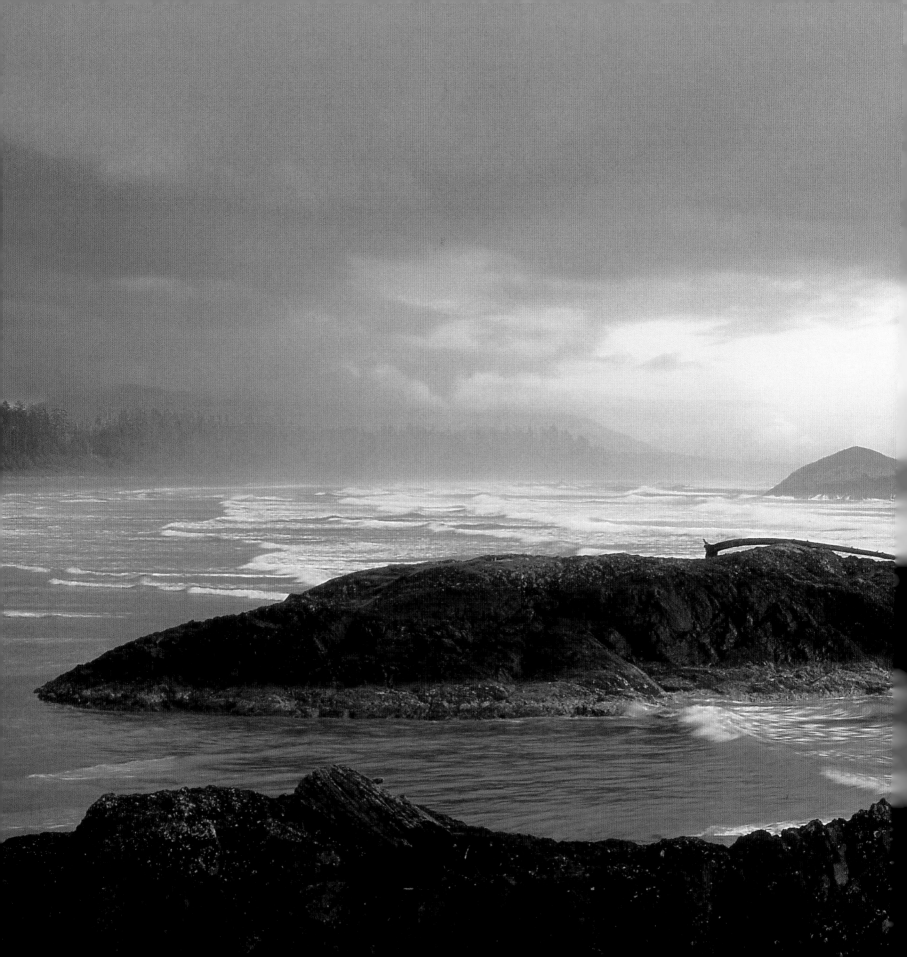

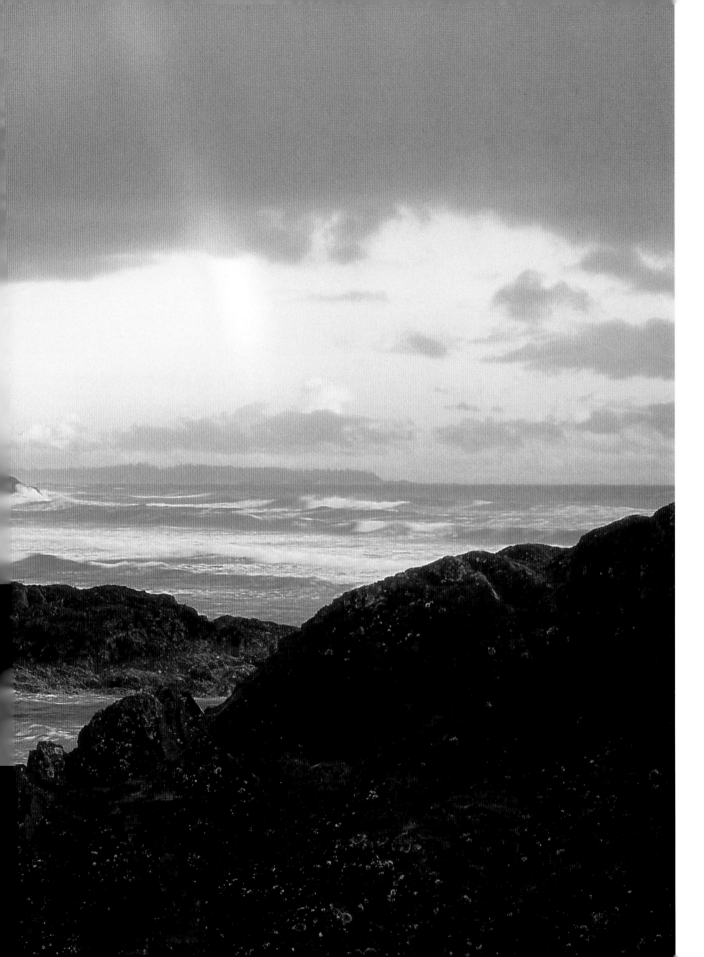

The Long Beach section of British Columbia's Pacific Rim National Park stretches for 30 kilometres south of Tofino on Vancouver Island. Harsh storms batter the shore each winter. In spring, visitors gather on the sand to watch for migrating grey whales.

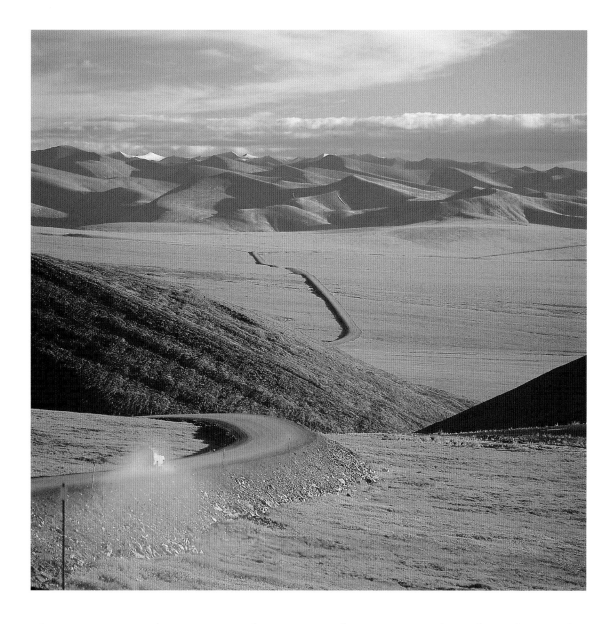

The Dempster Highway crosses the Arctic Circle on its route from the Yukon to the Northwest Territories. The highway is named after Corporal Dempster, the North-West Mounted Police officer who found the bodies of "the lost patrol," a team of four officers who died attempting the journey to Dawson City.

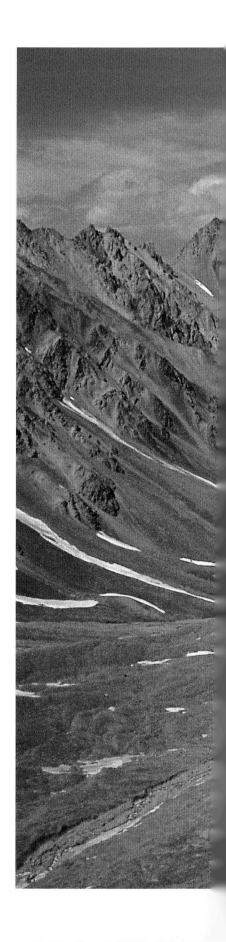

The Slims River Valley cuts through the towering mountains of Kluane National Park in the Yukon, which boasts the world's largest non-polar icefields. In contrast to these barren heights, the park's valleys harbour the greatest diversity of plants and birds north of the 60th parallel.

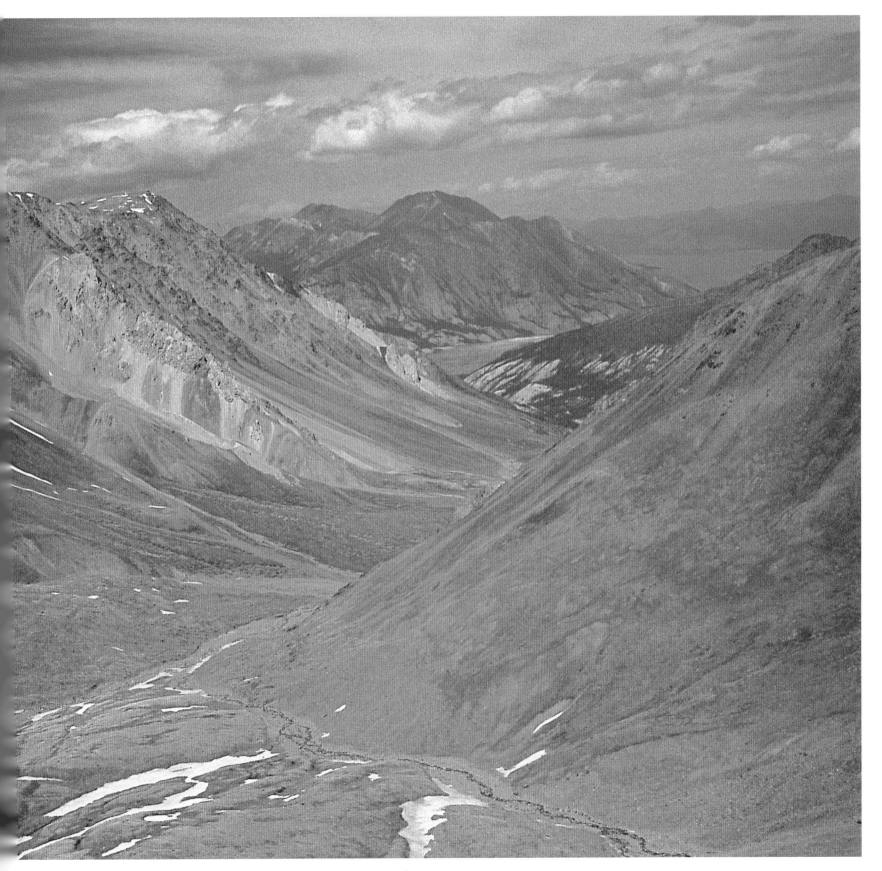

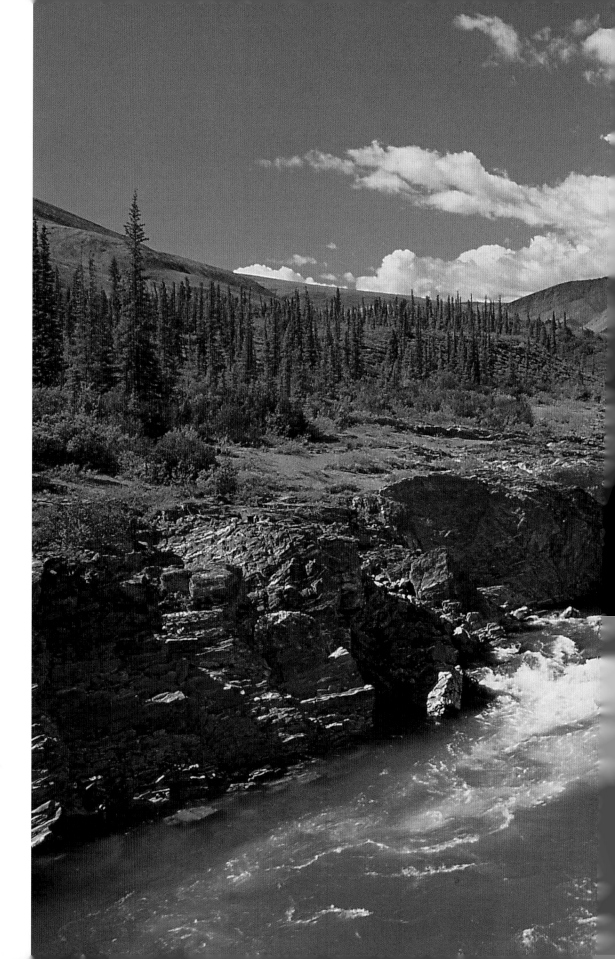

The icy Firth River rushes through Ivvavik National Park in the northern Yukon. *Ivvavik* means "nursery" in the language of area First Nations. The park is a birthing ground for thousands of caribou each spring when the world's largest caribou herd migrates to the area to calve.

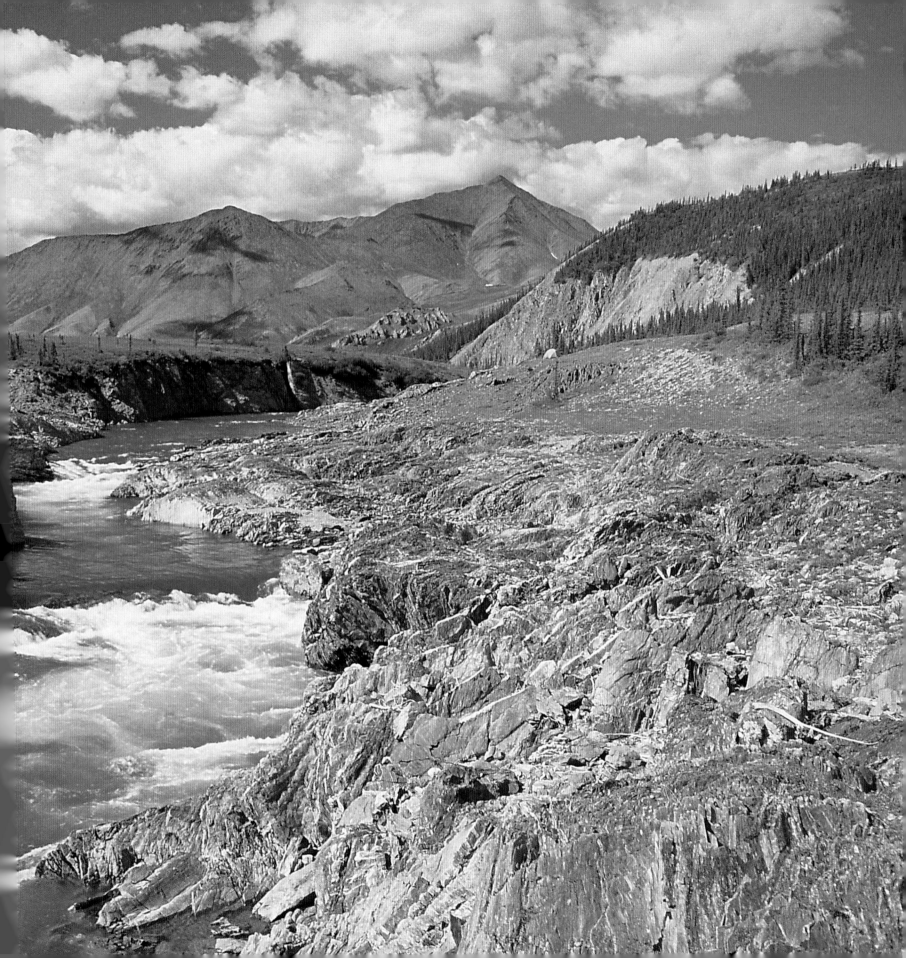

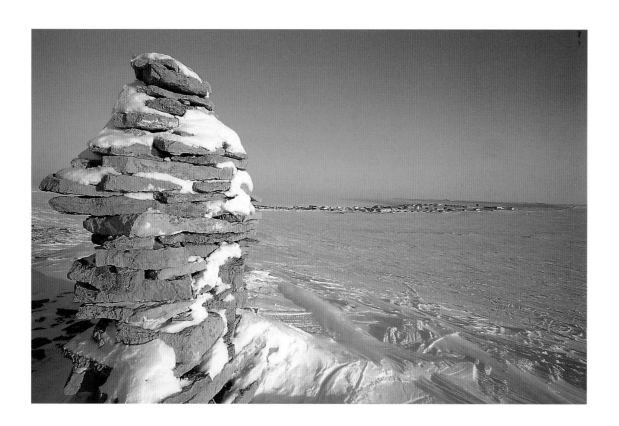

Where Baffin Island meets Foxe Basin, the boundary between land and water is marked only by the texture of the snow. The fifth-largest island in the world, Baffin lies on the western edge of Canada's Arctic Archipelago, only a few hundred kilometres from the shores of Greenland.

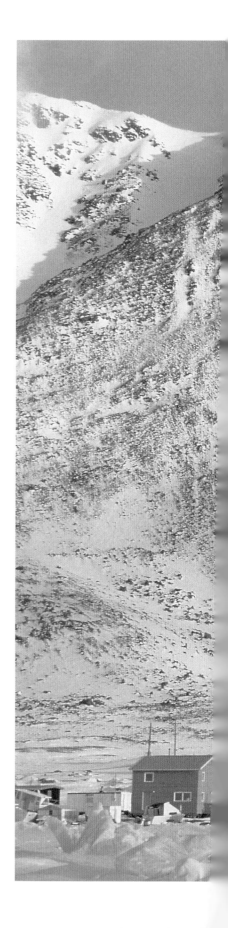

One of the most remote communities on earth, Grise Fiord is dwarfed by the bare mountains of Ellesmere Island, in Canada's Arctic. Despite the inhospitable climate, Grise Fiord is not the first of Ellesmere Island's settlements. First Nations hunters lived here more than 4000 years ago.

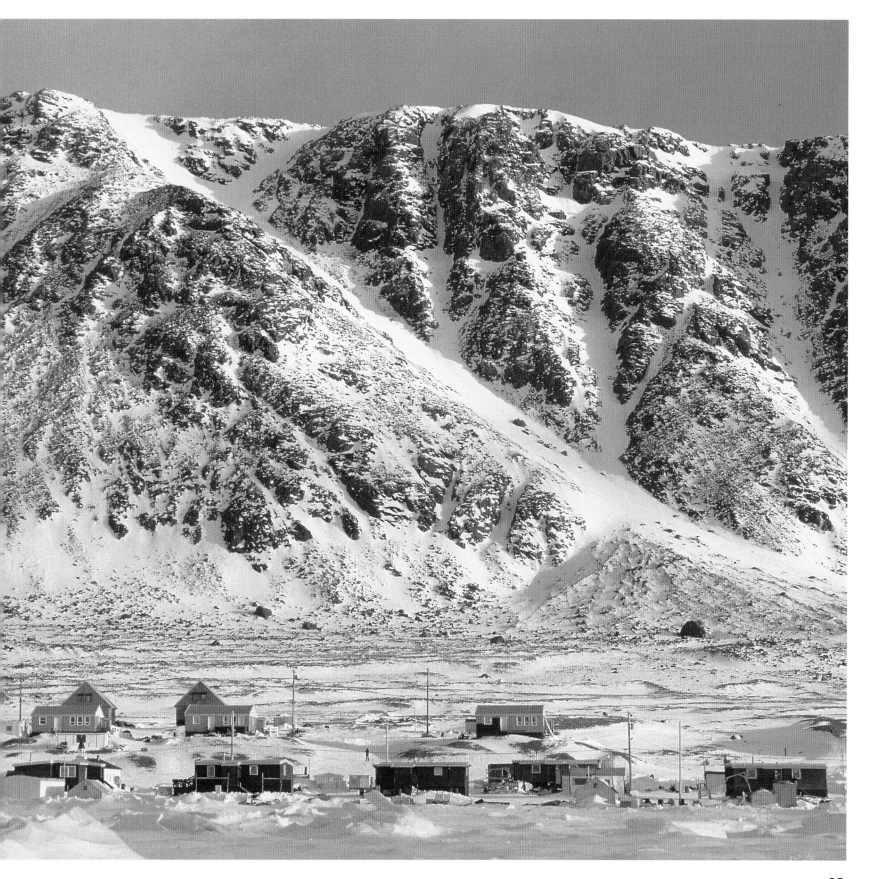

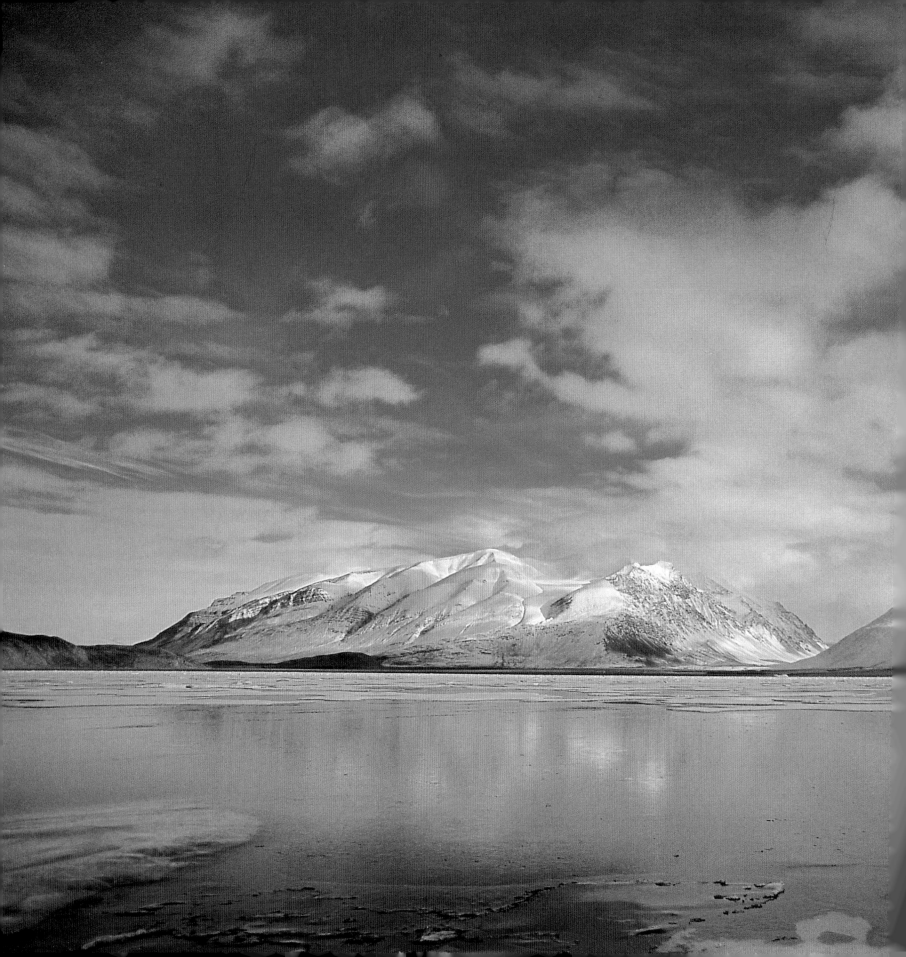

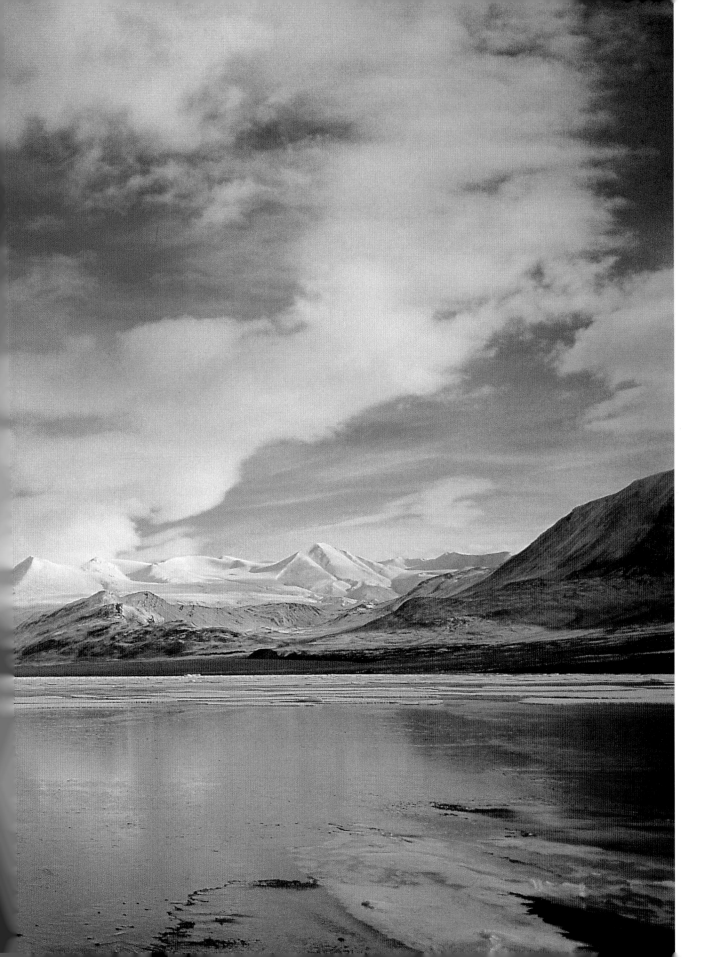

Ellesmere Island National Park, in Canada's Arctic, stretches for 37,775 square kilometres, more than six times the area of Prince Edward Island. Glaciers have carved the island into deep valleys and fiords, such as Tanquary Fiord. This area is free of frost for less than two months each year.

Photo Credits

M. GRANDMAISON i, iii, 55, 66

DARWIN WIGGETT 6–7, 10, 12–13, 59, 60

JOHN SYLVESTER/FIRST LIGHT 8, 9, 14, 15, 18, 19, 20–21, 22, 23, 25

KEN STRAITON/FIRST LIGHT 11, 34, 72–73

CHRIS CHEADLE/FIRST LIGHT 16–17, 84

THOMAS KITCHIN/FIRST LIGHT 24, 28, 29, 30, 35, 36, 69

VICTORIA HURST/FIRST LIGHT 26–27, 31

RON WATTS/FIRST LIGHT 32–33, 76, 78, 80–81

W. P. MCELLIGOTT/FIRST LIGHT 37

J. COCHRANE/FIRST LIGHT 38–39

BENJAMIN RONDEL/FIRST LIGHT 40–41, 46, 48–49

WAYNE LYNCH 42, 74-75, 90–91, 94–95

MICHAEL E. BURCH 43, 47

PIERRE GUEVREMONT/FIRST LIGHT 44–45

MARK BURNHAM/FIRST LIGHT 50–51

DAVE REEDE/FIRST LIGHT 52–53, 54, 62

MIKE GRANDMAISON/FIRST LIGHT 56

DARWIN WIGGETT/FIRST LIGHT 57, 61, 63, 64–65, 67, 70, 71

GLEN AND REBECCA GRAMBO/FIRST LIGHT 58

LARRY J. MACDOUGALL/FIRST LIGHT 68

CHRIS HARRIS/FIRST LIGHT 77

DAVID NUNUK/FIRST LIGHT 79

DOLORES BASWICK/FIRST LIGHT 82–83

ADAM GIBBS 85, 86–87

RICHARD HARTMIER/FIRST LIGHT 88

ALAN SIRULNIKOFF/FIRST LIGHT 89

ROBERT SEMENIUK/FIRST LIGHT 92

JERRY KOBALENKO/FIRST LIGHT 93